THE
SHABBY
CHIC
COLLECTION

THE SHABBY CHIC
COLLECTION

SHABBY CHIC

RACHEL ASHWELL'S SHABBY CHIC TREASURE HUNTING & DECORATING GUIDE

THE SHABBY CHIC HOME

RACHEL ASHWELL

ReganBooks
An Imprint of HarperCollinsPublishers

FOR JAKE AND LILLY

For *Shabby Chic:* Interior photographs and illustrations by Art Streiber. Interior design by Joel Avirom and Jason Snyder.

For *Rachel Ashwell's Shabby Chic Treasure Hunting & Decorating Guide:* Interior photographs and illustrations by Wynn Miller and Cathy Mogull; additional photographs on pages 5 and 46 through 47 by Rosalind Simon. Interior design by Gabrielle Raumberger Design, Santa Monica, California: Gabrielle Raumberger and Clifford Singontiko. The floral arrangements that appear in the photographs of Bountiful are courtesy of Brian Wark.

For *The Shabby Chic Home:* Interior photographs and illustrations by Amy Neunsinger. Interior design: Gabrielle Raumberger Design, Santa Monica, California: Gabrielle Raumberger and Clifford Singontiko and Charles Rue Woods; sketches and illustrations by Deborah Greenfield; text by Annabel Davis-Goff.

Printed on acid-free paper

ISBN 0-06-008312-3

01 02 03 04 05 RRD 10 9 8 7 6 5 4 3 2 1

SHABBY
CHIC

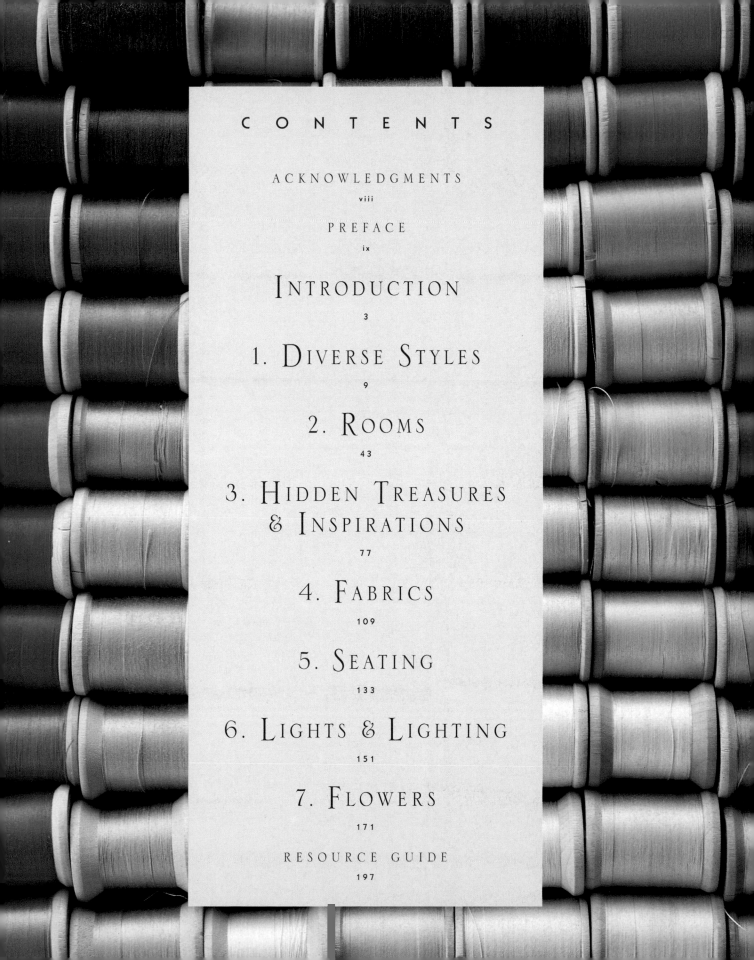

CONTENTS

ACKNOWLEDGMENTS

This book is a collaboration of many dear people and their support, enthusiasm, and knowledge.

First, my thanks to Ted, who helped me formulate and focus my thoughts, enabling me to express myself and discover what I didn't know I knew. If I hadn't had that ability, this book would have been very different.

I thank Glynis and Art for their expertise and their openness to understanding my so particular a vision.

I thank the loyalty and encouragement of Brendon McBreen and my Shabby Chic staff as well as all those clients who inspired me and allowed me to photograph their homes and possessions.

My thanks to Nina Krivanek for her gloriously refreshing floral displays. My gratitude to Judith Regan and Joseph Montebello, whose interest in Shabby Chic allowed for the book.

My thanks also to Luppe for the endless supply of beverages and laughter when we all became a little too serious.

And last, my many thanks to my parents, Shirley and Elliott Greenfield. They set examples for me of how to be comfortable with imperfections, and taught me that imperfections represent the traces of life that should be valued and respected, not covered up or discarded.

PREFACE

Shabby Chic evolved as a practical answer to family living. When I found myself a mother of two, in a world of sticky fingerprints and muddy shoe tracks, I began to throw rumpled white denim or cotton over my couches and chairs, as almost more of a whim or afterthought. Slipcovering my furniture wasn't a well-thought-out plan devised to protect my furniture, and it certainly wasn't something I invented. Yet there was a certain appeal to this sensible, washable, portable way of dealing with modern living, and soon my friends began asking for slipcovers for themselves. That is how Shabby Chic—the store—began.

Since then, Shabby Chic has evolved into furniture, fabrics, and home accessories that have the same casual appeal and easy style as slipcovers. It is a style that is quiet, simple, peaceful, and practical, allowing for the mixture of many tastes. It does not commit to Victorian, modern, or any other particular era and can work with a number of different styles or houses. Over the years I have learned that the house itself is of less importance than its contents and how those contents reflect the life within.

In my travels, many things have passed through my hands, but those few items that I hold on to are those with the character, wrinkles, and imperfections of history and experience. It is my hope that this book offers insight on knowing how to see these things, what makes them appealing and useful, and how they fit into the Shabby Chic style.

SHABBY
CHIC

INTRODUCTION

Comfort, the beauty of imperfection, the allure of time-worn objects, and the appeal of simple, practical living: These are the cornerstones of what has come to be known as the Shabby Chic style. Shabby Chic, the home furnishings label and retail chain I founded in 1989, is now recognized not only as a brand name, but as a decorating style. Though some may find the phrase "shabby chic"—the idea that something "shabby" (faded and dilapidated) can be considered "chic" (elegant and stylish)—paradoxical, the two elements go hand in hand. Shabbiness, in its shunning of what is too new, modern, or ostentatious, as well as in its rebellion against perfection, is precisely what makes this comfortable look so alluring. The cozy familiarity of a well-worn, beloved pair of faded blue jeans—versus the starched stiffness of a new pair—is the appeal of Shabby Chic.

I didn't invent this relaxed style. Europeans have long appreciated this approach to living: Witness the dilapidated elegance of an Italian villa, French castle, or English country estate whose owners can easily afford new furnishings, but prefer the worn grandeur of faded velvets and peeling vanities handed down from their ancestors. Shabby Chic represents a revived appreciation for what is useful, well loved, and comfortable, for those things that some might perceive as being too tattered and worn to be of use or value.

Collecting important, rare, or costly objects meant to be seen and not touched is not part of the Shabby Chic philosophy. My philosophy of decor is that nothing should be too precious. A child should feel free to put her feet on the sofa, a guest, his cup on the coffee table. I believe in cozy, not fussy; relaxed, not stiff. I believe in living in, on, and around one's things, not merely with them.

A roomy, slipcovered chair big enough for a child and a dog or two, with slightly wrinkled, worn fabric and ample arms perfect for plopping your legs over; an old trunk, its paint peeling around the edges, given new life as a coffee table; a vase of roses from the garden, a bit wilted, a few petals missing; a vintage mirror, framed with a white floral iron piece salvaged from an old gate and chipped in places, but still charming; a slightly rusted flea market chandelier; a scratched-up coal scuttle used as a bread box; an array of vanilla-scented candles adding a warm glow to a cozy room—these are some of the elements of the effortless, inviting look I prefer. Colors in keeping with this way of living tend to be soft, palatable tones such as seafoam, mint, and celadon greens; dusty roses; pale sky blues; and ivories, creams, and grays that appear to be muted by age, or crisp, clean whites that blend with everything. Brighter or darker colors can occasionally be a part of the look if they are treated with subtlety, combined with white or light colors, or if they appear to be faded by time.

But Shabby Chic goes far beyond the stereotype of a few tea-stained florals and some cushy chairs. Some have called this shabby yet elegant look "a marriage between the laid-back, breezy ease of Los Angeles beach life and the romantic prettiness of English country life at its most casual." Others have described it as having "the aura of old money, cushy comfort, and crafted indifference" or as "the merging of a romantic, old-fashioned, aesthetic appeal with modern functions." To these qualities, I would add that the style suggests things that are inherited rather than store-bought and handcrafted rather than mass-produced. It is also a style that is appreciative of the beauty of process and evolution.

I'm attracted to the quirky appeal of chips, stains, cracks, dents, and irregularities that assert character and reveal the charm of history. I gravitate toward the crumbling, the disheveled, the tattered, and the battered. I am drawn to materials that are happily vulnerable to the effects of time, weather, and touch, influences that result in discoloration, staining, tearing, shrinkage, and fading. But I also believe in function, eschewing waste, and in advocating new uses for old forms. In practical terms, this means using washable fabrics, recovering or restuffing an old sofa or chair instead of buying a new one, combining objects that are complementary rather than a perfect match (an approach that is especially handy if you are missing pieces of sets), and paring down as opposed to adding on. I have turned many an old door into a coffee table, crumbling moldings into picture frames, and wicker laundry hampers into end tables. I rarely discard anything that is serviceable and somewhat aesthetically pleasing without at least attempting to find a place and use for it.

Unlike some decorative styles that work only in certain types of environments, Shabby Chic is a style that is versatile and boundary free. As a design philosophy of comfort and faded splendor, it encompasses

BELOW: **Here is a good example of how flowers, in this case, ones made of painted leather, can be used to adorn common fixtures. Note how the cracks in the wall behind this beveled mirror echo the shabby feeling of the flowers.**

OPPOSITE: **I transformed this old coal scuttle I found at a flea market into a bread box simply by cleaning it up and adding a piece of white linen. The box could also be used for cookies, rice, pasta, or other dry foodstuffs.**

not only furniture and fabrics, but also the more subtle nuances of lighting, flowers, and color. This book will help you learn how you can easily incorporate this unaffected look of timeworn elegance and practicality into your own home. Here, I show you how the style works not only in traditional country homes and cozy beach cottages, but in high-tech contemporary houses and rented apartments where one is forced to work around certain unchangeable structures. I illustrate how different rooms—from bathrooms and bedrooms to eating areas and living rooms—respond to distinct elements of this style and suggest several ways to help these spaces achieve a simple and unpretentious style, sometimes by simply taking away clutter or by adding a touch as basic yet as luxurious as a basket of fluffy white towels. With a trip to the flea market, I demonstrate how to find treasures amid the trash, showing you what to look for and offering ideas on restoring and revamping. I emphasize the significance of furniture that highlights comfort, has classic appeal, and complements an entire look. I also point out the ways in which different fabrics can help to create a specific mood and stress the importance of using personal inspiration—from nature, life events, or even ordinary observations—to create a home with an individual, welcoming feel. The ephemeral beauty of flowers in all their stages, from the garden to fresh arrangement

ABOVE: I loved the rusty patina of this little iron end table I'm holding here at a flea market. All I did to make it functional was to top it with a piece of glass.

OPPOSITE: The intricacy of the ironwork on this Italian chair and table with an ivy motif indicates the pieces' age. Modern iron pieces tend to be much cruder. The worn patches on the leaves and the variations in color add to the authenticity and appeal of the furniture. (See Resource Guide.)

to falling, faded petals, as well as the way they are represented in paintings, on fabric, or on decorative objects, is also discussed.

Although I offer several helpful hints, this book is not a manual, but rather a detailed illustration of the various ways in which you can easily achieve your own version of the Shabby Chic style. The key lies in simply weeding out the unnecessary, trusting your instincts about what is comfortable and practical, noticing details, experimenting with new and complementary combinations of colors and fabrics, and looking at imperfection and age with a whole new appreciation for their unique significance and beauty.

1
DIVERSE
STYLES

What is essential to the relaxed, shabby yet chic look, marked by what is comfortable, worn, and often tattered, can be incorporated easily into a variety of decorating styles. A cushy, white slipcovered chair, a casual floral arrangement, a peeling vintage piece, soft lighting, the use of white, and mixed and matched fabrics and textures can look as natural in a sleek, contemporary home as they do in a more traditional setting, such as an eclectic Spanish, French country, or casual beach house. Making the style work is a simple matter of how the elements are put together.

The key to making everything work is to include a balance of complements and contrasts, a display of the effects of time, traces of real life, and a merging of gilt and grit. Anything that appears too contrived or calculated is the antithesis of this look. The Shabby Chic style opts for haphazard arrangements over perfectly symmetrical ones, framed pictures propped against walls rather than hung neatly, and rumpled fabrics rather than pressed finishes.

There are certain floor, wall, and ceiling treatments that I consider to be effective foundations for the Shabby Chic look. Sisal rugs, tile, and hardwood floors, for example, work in formal and casual settings and with a variety of furniture styles, be they traditional or contemporary. White and off-white walls, textured wallpaper, interesting molding treatments, and natural cracks and crumbles can work in almost any style home, as can high, exposed wooden beam or embossed tin ceilings.

While there are certain elements that work with most style homes, such as white slipcovered chairs, there are certain variations that work better for some styles than others. In a high-tech contemporary home, for example, fitted slipcovers may work better with the sleek surroundings than would the loose and roomy look more typical of the Shabby Chic style. Whereas, in a beach house, a casual, more rumpled look blends in better with the overall relaxed mood. Following are some specific examples of how basic elements of the Shabby Chic style, as well as modifications of the look, work in different homes from modern to traditional.

PREVIOUS PAGES: This bedroom is composed of a series of misfit pieces. Nothing quite matches, but everything manages to blend into a comfortable mix of soft creams and pinks. I've managed to ignore the crudeness of the Levelor blinds and nylon carpet—aspects that are fixed by virtue of the beach house being a rental—by simply working around them. Children's artwork is the only wall decor. The daybed, to which I added comfortable neck rolls, does double duty as a refuge for the kids when they wander in in the middle of the night. (See Resource Guide.)

OPPOSITE: This vintage crystal beaded chandelier, the rumpled silk fabric, rusty white table leg, and slightly withered linen flowers in a tarnished mercury vase all represent the less than perfect look of Shabby Chic.

CASUAL BEACH

y rented seafront home is an example of how unchangeable structures can be worked around and strong points (such as picture windows with ocean views) played up. It also shows how pieces with a bit of faded grandeur can add a touch of elegance to a casual beach environment. Because the home is a rental, I did what I could, covering the existing ugly carpets with sisal rugs and adding simple white Roman shades to the windows, while ignoring elements like aluminum window trim, louvered blinds, and unsightly light-switch covers. Because I prefer a subdued look, every room is done in a monochromatic scheme of muted and sun-bleached floral prints. Cushy slipcovered seating is paired with crumbling, painted vintage or wicker furniture. Floral-motif accessories and paintings are combined with wrought-iron chandeliers or wicker lamps. Fresh, but not perfect, garden flowers and my children's artwork add unique personal touches.

LEFT: Fine details are crucial indicators of a piece's quality. The intricate wood-carved detailing on the molding of this old bar mirror belies the frame's age, marking it with value not easily matched in newer pieces. The play of shapes—an oval mirror in a rectangular frame—adds interest, too. The piece complements the muted mustard sideboard, also characterized by carved detailing. Fresh peonies and porcelain candleholders emphasize the flower carvings and add color.

OPPOSITE: A delicate blend of different elements—light, fabric, texture, and color—make the difference between a functional corner and a functional yet inviting one. A combination of candles and early morning light imbue this cozy living room alcove in my beach house with a soft tranquillity. The muted seafoam greens, creams, and whites echo the tones of the ocean and sand outside, while wicker, wood, and fabric blur into a harmony of textures. A vintage piece of lace placed over the back of a slipcovered chair hides the inevitable sticky fingerprint left by a child. Sisal rugs cover the drab carpet, and a vintage pitcher and glass decorated with painted flowers offer cool refreshment. (See Resource Guide.)

Flowers—both real and represented—are
the unifying theme in the living room of my
beach house. Toile candleholders and floral
paintings expand upon the mood set by the
large and small rose-print fabrics used for
the slipcovered sofa and chair. Petals from a
fresh arrangement of roses that have fallen
to the tabletop are left to stay, adding to the
room's melancholy, peaceful feel. Because
the tones are a monochromatic blend of
seafoam, sage, olive, and celadon greens and
cream, the look is prevented from appearing
too busy or romantic. (See Resource Guide.)

CONTEMPORARY

In a contemporary home in Venice, California, with its living room of marble, modern shapes, and slick surfaces, an inviting slipcovered sofa and chair break up the starkness and offer warmth. In keeping with the house's streamlined style, however, the slipcovers are more fitted than the usual Shabby Chic loose and roomy style and can be dry-cleaned rather than laundered to maintain their sleek look. Other worn yet stylish additions that offset the home's high-tech look are slightly worn vintage pieces and rugged textures, such as an ornate iron gate converted into a coffee table. Quirky antique fixtures and accessories merge the old with the new and give the polished bathroom a less inaccessible feel, as the photos on these pages show.

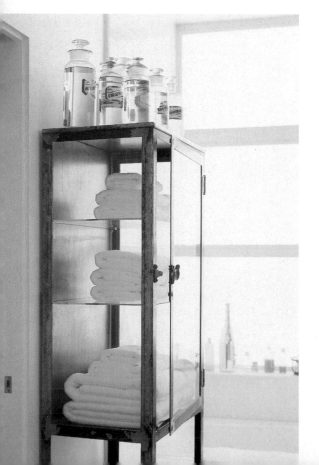

LEFT: In sleek, contemporary settings such as this, a touch of the old can add comfort and approachability. In this modern California bathroom, a vintage dentistry cabinet and chemist's bottles introduce the patina of old textures and shapes to alleviate the starkness. These items are functional, too: The cabinet is used to store stacks of fresh white towels and the bottles to hold shampoos, oils, and lotions. In full view, the contents themselves are objects to be appreciated aesthetically. (See Resource Guide.)

ABOVE: Native American stone bowls echo the granite floors and hard gray walls of this contemporary house. The intricate wrought-iron table salvaged from an old gate lends texture; the flowers, softness; and the fruit, color to the surroundings. (See Resource Guide.)

OPPOSITE: The slipcovered furniture in this modern house adds an element of comfort, but is fitted and modern in shape in keeping with the room's sleek mood. I also covered the table with a high-gloss white finish and topped it with a sheet of glass rather than let the rust and chips of this iron tabletop show through, as I usually would. (See Resource Guide.)

TRADITIONAL

The Mediterranean-style home of film director Tony Scott and his wife, Donna, though traditional and somewhat formal in style, is made more approachable with the introduction of vintage Italian wall sconces, crackled moldings used as mirror frames, slipcovered furniture (though of a formal fabric and fitted tightly), pillows made from antique textiles, and scuffed wicker. These worn and comfortable pieces merge with the Scott's collection of formal antiques, lacquered pieces, fine oil paintings, precious rugs, and chandeliers in a way that retains their grandeur while rendering them less pristine. Framed family photographs lend a personal touch, and loose, gardenlike floral bouquets, rather than stiffly composed arrangements, are used to further maintain a relaxed atmosphere.

LEFT: When decorative objects have no real function other than beauty, an element of whimsy can make surrounding expensive, formal pieces feel more approachable. This delicate Goldscheider bust on the mantel in Tony and Donna Scotts' formal living room attracted the couple because of its mischievous expression.

BELOW: Important pieces and formal trappings do not have to make a room feel unlivable. The Scotts' octagon-shaped living room is filled with precious works of art, a grand piano, nineteenth-century French oil paintings, and an Aubusson carpet, yet it maintains an inviting, comfortable atmosphere. The starkness of the room's black lacquer pieces is offset by the coziness of slipcovered chairs and sofas, personal photographs, casual flower arrangements, and pillows made of antique textiles. (See Resource Guide.)

Talent manager Sandy Gallin's Malibu home overlooking the Pacific Ocean has a classic New England-meets-California look. Furnished somewhat formally with dark antiques and dark wood floors, hoards of hard-bound books, handcrafted carpets, formal oil paintings, and a grand piano, the house feels semicasual and inviting due to the predominance of deep, white denim and Marseilles slipcovered chairs and sofas in every room. Gallin and his longtime decorator, Bill Lane, installed these luxurious chairs and couches not only in the living room, den, library, bedroom, and guest house, but in the bathrooms, screening room, and gym, too. "The white slipcovered effect comes from both Sandy's love of the Hamptons look and also because [the slipcovers] are practical—he lives at the beach and he has three dogs," says Lane. "Sandy is also very consistent. Not very many people would do every room in their house in the same colors—dark wood, some green velvet, and white furniture, but in this case it absolutely works." Another presence in every room is Gallin's flower of choice, orchids, which, while echoing the house's rather formal atmosphere, bring life, the outdoors, and color into the somewhat monochromatic scheme.

The Malibu home of talent manager Sandy Gallin illustrates how the formal and the traditional can be made more casual for California beach living with the use of roomy chairs and sofas, slipcovers made of white denim, and old Marseilles bedcovers. With the help of his interior designer, Bill Lane, Gallin has created an elegant simplicity, remaining faithful to white throughout, including chairs, sofas, towels, and dishes. The generous use of white also adds light to the dark wood antique furniture. OPPOSITE: A corner of the library.

PAGES 24–25: The master bedroom.

PAGES 26–27: Oftentimes, it's the unexpected that makes the difference between an ordinary room and a spectacular one. Rather than traditional theater seats, Gallin's screening room has two tiers of plush white denim slipcovered couches. Further personalizing the room is a large photograph of Gallin's pug dogs, which drops down during screenings to reveal the projection booth, old-fashioned jars filled with candy for guests' enjoyment, and orchids, which add life and color.

ECLECTIC

ny home can be transformed to express its owner's personal statement. Homes that integrate several different looks and reveal their owners' interests and tastes are far preferable to homes that appear too planned, look too professionally decorated, or where decor is enslaved by theme.

The Spanish-style home of interior stylist Philomena Giusti demonstrates how the cluttered, eclectic look can be successful. Giusti's house is brimming with examples of new uses for old forms and with items that may seem shabby but have great style, making the formal casual and the casual formal, and bringing the outdoors in. The key is that all of the pieces have character and function, hold special meaning for Giusti, and have been put together in an interesting way.

A peeling Mexican bar is used as a kitchen cabinet, an inexpensive lace curtain as a tablecloth. Chairs are mismatched. Checked fabrics are mixed

ABOVE: Though pieces in the casual, comfortable Shabby Chic style are usually as much about function as they are about form, objects without a real purpose that add life or create a distinct mood are desirable, too. This Roman-style statue standing guard over Philomena Giusti's front rose garden sets a gentle, welcoming tone.

RIGHT: In the living room of Giusti's Spanish-style home a cushy antique red sofa adds a shock of color, an antique zebra rug lends a note of old-world whimsy, and a worn leather chair with a velvet cushion offers a cozy corner to relax in. Eighteenth-century Italian angels tucked into niches over the fireplace stand guard over the room, along with oil paintings of women dating from the twenties and thirties that Giusti believes resemble her mother and sister. A scattering of plants and fresh roses from the garden bring the outdoors in.

with florals throughout the house. Old leather armchairs and chipped iron sconces are allowed to proudly flaunt the effects of time and wear. Chandeliers become less imposing when used in the bathroom and garden, and silver less formal when used for a casual snack atop an old wine taster's table. Rusted patio and wicker furniture, garden plants and statues are brought inside to blur the distinction between indoors and out. The house contains a wealth of personal objects that Giusti has collected over time, including the worn and cracked hands and feet of statues, vintage oil portraits that she rests against the wall rather than hangs, and family photographs displayed in an array of antique frames. "There's no real rhyme or reason to what's here or where it's placed," says Giusti. "It's not about what country or which era anything's from. It's about what I like, which is pieces with character. And it's definitely not about matching."

TOP LEFT: This weathered head from a garden statue, which rests peacefully in a planter inside Philomena Giusti's living room, illustrates how pieces meant for the outdoors can work just as well indoors.

CENTER AND BOTTOM LEFT: Objects that show the ravages of time have their own beauty, and parts of an object can be as attractive as the whole. The delicacy and sense of decay of this broken hand and pair of tiny chipped feet from an antique statue attracted Giusti.

OPPOSITE: Eating in the kitchen used to be a practice reserved for servants and children, but this room is now considered a favorite place for informal gatherings in many homes. The colorful food, bright sunflowers, and mismatched plates and napkins add to the eclectic, friendly clutter of Giusti's kitchen. A toile chandelier from the forties sheds soft light on a worn farmer's table surrounded by stools covered in a vintage vegetable-print fabric. In the background, a decaying green cabinet houses neatly stacked dishes, while a floral pillow blends easily with a casual red and white striped wooden chair.

The eclectic Topanga Canyon home of Chantall Cloutier, owner of the hair, makeup, and style agency by her name, also incorporates some basics of the Shabby Chic style. In this case, white walls, white slipcovered chairs and couches, and a coffee table fashioned from a vintage door painted white all serve as backdrops for Cloutier's plush velvet throws, pillows, and curtains in deep jewel tones. The introduction of white prevents the richness of the rest of the furnishings from becoming overbearing. "I love white," says Cloutier. "It's so versatile. A different color couch wouldn't allow me to make changes as easily and I'm constantly changing and rearranging."

Cloutier allows the style of her house to evolve, adding and subtracting pieces she collects at flea markets, auctions, and vintage and antique shops. Her somewhat theatrical bathroom illustrates how merging the formal with the casual and using the element of surprise can transform a room into something that is unpredictable yet comfortable and functional. Mirrors are used to create the illusion of more space. An overstuffed, slipcovered armchair and Turkish rugs helped turn the area into a plush sitting room of sorts. A bust, oil paintings, and a gilded towel rack made from a vintage pedestal—all picked up at flea markets—are whimsical yet formal additions that enhance the room's unique feel. Throughout the house are many windows that Cloutier had installed to lighten the look of her gilded mirrors and frames, columns, and dark fabrics.

LEFT: An old theater curtain in burgundy velvet draped in loose swags lends formality to this eclectic corner in Chantall Cloutier's home. The stark white piano is offset by the dark velvets of the antique chair, blue pillow, piano bench cover, curtains, and custom-made lamp shade. An array of personal objects—silver frames, a mirror, floral painting, red roses, and a candelabrum—carry through the theatrical theme.

OPPOSITE: Cloutier's home office is luxurious yet very functional. The ornate, carved wooden desk is made from an old table topped with glass. The bookends are a new use for rose-motif fireplace andirons. The lamps, flea market finds, have custom-made lamp shades. The vintage carved wooden mirror creates a sense of light and space.

FOLLOWING PAGES: The Topanga Canyon bathroom exemplifies the idea of creating the unexpected. Five mirrors, several windows, and French doors leading to a garden add to the spacious feeling of this already large bathroom, where Cloutier created an indoor-outdoor mood. An overstuffed armchair made from different tablecloths sewn together, an angel towel rack, and reproduction Turkish rugs transform the space into an almost luxurious sitting room. Tiled floors, walls, and door trim add an aesthetic as well as a practical touch.

THE COMPONENTS
OF STYLE

Time-worn furniture, crinkled fabrics, muted colors, and imperfect chandeliers or cracked paintings may be the mainstays of Shabby Chic decor, but before combining them to create an overall ambiance for a room, there are other, more basic components to be dealt with. The structure of the room itself, in the form of its floors, walls, and ceilings all need to be considered before, or at least in conjunction with, tackling its contents. The following section points out which of these elemental components blends best with the kinds of pieces that define the Shabby Chic style, whatever the architectural style of the house.

Floor, wall, and ceiling treatments are the basis of every home's style and ambiance. These three components are often noticed on a more subtle rather than overt level, but they create a world of difference in setting an atmosphere. The contrast between a hardwood floor and wall-to-wall carpeting, paneled and clean white walls, and high and low ceilings illustrates how vital these basic elements are to a room. The way they are treated makes a vast difference as to whether they will serve as backdrops or take a more active role in a room's actual appeal.

Although floor, wall, and ceiling treatments can be done after a room's fabrics, furniture, and accessories have been selected, I find that using these three surfaces as a starting point is the easiest way to go about decorating a home.

FLOORS

When it comes to floors, I believe first and foremost in simplicity of look and ease of care. Floor coverings that create the most relaxed yet classic appearance include hardwood floors, sisal rugs, variations of Spanish or Mexican tile, and sandblasted cement. Floor coverings might set up a pleasing contrast with the rest of the house's look, for example, a sisal rug in a formal living room lends a touch of the casual. Or a floor may act as a complement to the surroundings, as a sandblasted cement floor would in a very modern home. These floorings also work best with the furniture and fabrics I prefer.

Hardwood floors work with almost any style furniture and are relatively easy to keep clean. Hardwood is generally more expensive than carpeting, typically costing six to thirty dollars per square foot, depending on the

wood. Preassembled hardwood floors that are glued down are slightly less expensive, costing about five dollars per square foot, but they are less flexible in terms of sanding, sealing, and staining. In some cases, you may want to put down a waterproof barrier between your hardwood covering and the floor—a professional can give you advice. I also like to add throw rugs to hardwood environments, as the additional color and pattern create a cozy appeal.

Sisal rugs have become increasingly popular. Made of natural root fibers woven in a ropelike fashion, they tend to give rooms a casual, almost indoor-outdoor feel. Most sisals are bound by rubber and backed by latex to make them more cushiony.

The tricky thing about sisals is that they're not that simple to care for. They absorb spills quickly and can easily ravel and pull. They also come in bolts that are typically twelve feet wide, so if a room is wider than this, other strips of sisal need to be added carefully along the sides to make the seams invisible.

Tiles, referred to by professionals as pavers, are great choices for kitchens, entryways, and bathrooms, but they also work well in dining and living rooms. Terra-cotta tiles in nine- to twelve-inch squares are relatively inexpensive. Fancier, imported tiles are much costlier, and marble even costlier, depending on its

quality. Typically, a mudpack—a base of roofing paper, chicken wire, then mortar or cement—needs to be laid down as a foundation for tile. This should be done professionally.

Sandblasted cement has become a common floor covering choice for many modern retailers. I used sandblasted cement in my Santa Monica shop because I like the cool patina it emanates, but it can also work well in residential situations. Sandblasting is a process that removes the creamy top layering of a cement floor to expose the rougher, sandy layer just below the surface, creating a textured appeal. Sandblasting machines can be easily rented, but keep in mind that the wear and tear that sandblasting can put on a house is tremendous. Everything must be removed, and walls and windows must be carefully protected with thick blankets.

WALLS

White walls are the most classic, clean foundations for any room. Acting as a sort of blank canvas, white complements and contrasts with a variety of colors, tones, and textures and serves well as a backdrop for all styles of furniture. Pure white, however, can be stark, so I prefer off-whites, eggshells, ivories, and creams. I often paint wall trimmings in a slightly different hue from the rest of the wall so that they stand out.

Like the humble appeal of a dresser with peeling paint or a leather chair with worn patches, imperfections in walls can be beautiful. Before rushing to cover natural cracks or crumbles with plaster or paint, take a good look at any flaws to discern whether they add charm and character.

Treatments such as wainscoting or anaglypta wallpaper (an embossed paper with a raised pattern) are other ways I like to add detailing to walls. These particular details tend to work best in homes that are traditional or old-fashioned in mood rather than in sleek, contemporary ones. In bathrooms, kitchens, and dining rooms, tongue-and-groove wood slats (they fit together like puzzle pieces) that extend from floor to chair height add texture. The slats are also functional, protecting the wall from banging chairs. When finished in high-gloss paint, wainscoting is easier to wash than regular walls. I installed a wainscoting of tongue-and-groove slats in my old bathroom for just these reasons.

Anaglypta adds texture and detail to a wall without overpowering it. Though it is applied like wallpaper, true anaglypta comes only in white and without a finished surface. Anaglypta must be painted (even if you repaint it white), otherwise spills will seep right through. As with wainscoting, I use semi- or high-gloss paint on anaglypta because it's very washable. Anaglypta is most often used for only the bottom half of a wall and is typically separated from the painted top portion by a chair rail or wood molding (I prefer moldings at least three inches thick to create a stronger demarcation). Some types of anaglypta can be purchased for as little as twelve dollars for a twenty- to twenty-five-square-foot roll.

This anaglypta wallpaper shows how a plain wall can become decorative in and of itself rather than simply serve as a backdrop for other pieces. Anaglypta—or embossed paper with a raised pattern—common at the turn of the century, can still be found at better wallpaper stores.

Wall and ceiling trimmings such as crown moldings (used at the junction of wall and ceiling), friezes (a band just under the crown molding), and other architectural ornaments can also be lovely decorative additions to a room. Most lumberyards offer a variety of standard wall moldings, but outlets specializing in architectural ornaments that look like carved wooden or plaster relief but are actually a special type of claylike dough offer a more interesting variety. Shaped and molded with heat and water, these ornaments are then steamed and bonded to a surface. They can also be glued with regular white glue to wood, metal, plaster, paint, or wallpaper, but steaming creates a better bonding effect. This little-known process dates back to sixteenth-century Italy, and the ornaments, referred to as composition ornaments, or compos, are common sights in elegant old hotels, theaters, and grand estates.

Composition ornaments are available in hundreds of different patterns, from columns, curves, and swirls to fleurs de lis, flowers, lions, urns, and cupids. The ornaments can be used as trim for walls, windows, floor edges, and ceilings as well as on furniture and fireplaces. Though I prefer original carvings on furniture rather than additions, compo has the ability to blend in easily as part of a piece and is more detailed than newer wood carvings. (I have occasionally used new compo pieces to add detailing to mirrors and frames.) Because it is semiperishable and becomes brittle over time, compo should be used no later than a month after it is ordered—the fresher it is when used, the better.

CEILINGS

High ceilings, especially those of exposed wood or wooden beams, while not always possible to achieve, are my choice for every style of home. But even if a room doesn't have a high ceiling, you can turn what exists into something more than an overhead covering and make it a prominent part of the decor of the space. Detailing such as medallions and rosettes—architectural ornaments that hold or surround light fixtures—and other trims

Stamped tin ceilings, which were very common at the turn of the century, are making a comeback. This one, at my Santa Monica store, is intricately detailed and was placed together piece by piece. Though expensive (this ceiling, which covers a three-thousand-square-foot area, cost four thousand dollars for materials and an additional four thousand dollars for installation), they come in a variety of patterns and completely transform a plain room into something grand.

are the types of touches that make a ceiling noticeable.

My favorite way to make a ceiling into something really special is to cover it with sheets of embossed or stamped tin. Common at the turn of the century and still found in old country stores, courthouses, and other buildings, embossed or stamped tin can still be purchased from a few outlets that have been in the business for years (see Resource Guide). Though expensive, tin ceilings, with their intricate designs, are truly beautiful. While you can hang tin ceilings yourself for about half the cost of having a professional do it for you, it's a complicated process requiring the installation of a dropped grid or acoustic framework. This is why I highly recommend using a professional contractor. Once installed, the ceiling needs to be painted. I use a pale color such as cream or mint green to prevent the ceiling from seeming too heavy.

Whether sisal rug or hardwood floor, plain white walls or embossed wallpaper, wooden beam or tin ceiling, the unifying characteristic of environments that work best with comfortable and worn Shabby Chic decor is simplicity. While floors, walls, and ceilings can certainly be interesting in their own right, I look at them more as backdrops to highlight a room's pieces. Overly decorated, colorful, or patterned structures not only detract from the interior furnishings of a room, but they also have less versatility and longevity. Neutral colors and plain or subtle textures have a longer lifespan and blend easily with any style home or specific space—living room, bathroom, or bedroom.

The next chapter addresses the particulars of these rooms from the functional to the aesthetic and explains how different approaches can be taken to imbue them with a Shabby Chic ambiance beyond floor, wall, and ceiling.

2

ROOMS

Every room in the home serves a specific purpose, so the decor of each must be approached individually. Focusing on the particular function of a room is an important first step in deciding how to decorate it. Whether a room is meant to be a private or social area, a place for work or for rest, and whether it will incur a little or a great deal of foot traffic are all factors that influence everything from fabric choice to furniture style and placement to lighting.

There are certain basic guidelines, however, that apply to every room. When I approach a room that needs to be redecorated, I sometimes empty out the contents to get a fresh perspective, then work my way back again. I may reinstall some of the items I took away, but I find that it's helpful to start with a blank slate. While I'm a firm believer in less being more, I'm also an advocate of recycling rather than discarding, so before throwing an item away, I consider whether or not it can be cleaned up, reupholstered, repainted, or given new hardware (see Chapter 3, "Hidden Treasures and Inspirations"). With regard to acces-

PREVIOUS PAGES: This exquisite, five-piece antique French bedroom set was one of my biggest splurges. The pale green bed, vanity, bedside table, oval table, and small table in the window are all marked by painstaking detail and attention to proportion. Every piece is dovetailed, and every curve, edge, and leg is indicative of fine craftsmanship. The tables are topped in gray marble, with ogee, or layered-effect, edges. The vanity mirror is mottled but not to the point of distortion, and all the pieces with drawers include keyholes and keys instead of knobs. With the needlepoint carpet, crystal chandelier, and French leather camelback chairs, the entire atmosphere exudes a faded Old World elegance. (See Resource Guide.)

TOP LEFT: Here, fragrant green plants in iron urns and a stack of white towels on an antique chair add freshness to what otherwise might have been a stuffy corner.

LEFT: What prompted me to buy this pale green table has everything to do with its detailing. The curvy shape of the legs, the casters, the tapered proportions, the marble top, and the bottom shelf with its intricate center ornament are all indications of quality. (See Resource Guide.)

OPPOSITE: A mix of silk, linen, lace, satin, and cotton give depth and luxuriousness to this vintage bed. The duvet is made of old Indian saris. (See Resource Guide.)

sories, I like to use them sparingly. Some clutter can be fine for very eclectic houses with lots of personal collections, but generally, I prefer a simple, clean, unfussy look.

If you're starting from scratch and need to buy almost every piece for a room, take your time and let the room evolve slowly. Allowing for such evolution always looks more natural, creates more character, and provides for the possibility that your tastes might change slightly over time. I find that rooms put together too quickly often look artificially decorated.

Sometimes a specific focal point—a fireplace or a picture window—is an obvious point of departure from which to base a room's particular arrangement. Other times, the focus of a room can be created by installing a large or dominant piece, such as a rug, couch, painting, or grand mirror.

BEDROOMS

Bedrooms should convey warmth, comfort, luxury, and intimacy. Bedrooms are where we begin and end our day—they ease us into the next phase of our daily schedules—and for that reason they shouldn't have too many distractions or too much clutter. In bedrooms, elements that bring on stress should be minimal—a work desk, a television, or a fax machine, for example, are better left for other rooms.

Since the bed itself is the focal point of most bedrooms, bedding is crucial. No matter its size or style, a bed should be an inviting sanctuary. Plenty of luscious layers—sheets, blankets, and goose-down duvets are the best way to make a bed luxurious, while comfort is the primary consideration when choosing cottons, flannels, or linens (see also Chapter 4, "Fabrics").

Crisp, clean white always looks and feels freshest when it comes to bedding, though, of course, color has its place. Mixing and matching patterns with pillows and quilts can create eye-catching contrasts in color and texture, while bed skirts are a way of adding detailing via ruffles.

Vintage headboards are one way to instill an element of faded grandeur. I often pick up dilapidated wooden architectural pieces at salvage yards and flea markets and turn them into headboards. It doesn't matter if these pieces are slightly larger than the bed—the extra bits at each end can serve as backdrops for end tables, as does the wooden headboard on my own bed.

In addition to the bed, seating is an important element of both formal and casual bedrooms. Chairs and love seats not only offer nonbed options for lounging with a book, they are also great temporary holding areas for clothes and bags. Since my bedroom is a gathering place for the whole family, I put in lots of cozy seating. My children love to curl up on the big slipcovered chair in the corner of the room or sprawl on the floral-print chaise lounge across from my bed.

Bringing in a bit of the outdoors—such as white wrought-iron garden furniture or a potted flowering plant—can also be a nice touch in the bedroom. And if you do a bedroom along a particular theme, such as florals, I suggest keeping the approach subtle.

OPPOSITE: This ragged old piece of wood that was once part of a gate now functions as a headboard in my bedroom. What made the piece worth unearthing at a salvage yard was its detailed wreath carving. That the headboard is larger than the bed is not a distraction. In fact, its size is an unexpected benefit that lets it serve as a backdrop for the end table. (See Resource Guide.)

French iron garden furniture brings in the mood of the
outdoors to Philomena Giusti's romantic bedroom. Rather
than adding a predictable piece of glass to the tabletop, Giusti
put in a mirror and placed white lacy pillows on the chairs to
give the pieces a boudoirlike feeling.

BATHROOMS

Clean, simple, private, luxurious, and practical: These are the words that best describe a Shabby Chic bathroom. The basics of any bathroom should be functional fixtures that provide plenty of space for displaying toiletries, towels, and other bits and bobs. For bathroom storage space, I suggest vintage vanities or flea market cabinets. Bathrooms can also be the perfect space for incorporating unexpected, glamorous touches such as old chandeliers, busts, painted mirrors, or fancy footstools.

Unusual containers for soaps, oils, salts, cotton balls, and hand towels are another way to lend individual touches to a bathroom. Large stone bowls, wire baskets, apothecary jars, wooden boxes, and fish bowls all make great repositories for sundries.

If a bathroom is large enough, cozy, roomy, slipcovered chairs can be the ultimate luxury, providing a loungelike quality, regardless of whether the space is formal or casual. For overly sleek contemporary bathrooms, I like to introduce offbeat vintage pieces, such as scruffy old, but cleaned, dentist's chests or medicine bottles, whose character and a sense of age act to offset the cool, polished tone.

Fresh stacks of plush towels on hand—preferably in white—are a welcome luxury, as are bountiful piles of pretty soaps. Tile and marble are terrific finishes for bathroom walls and floors, but if the floor is too cold, add a throw rug or two for warmth.

Apothecary jars used for cotton balls, cotton swabs, and other sundries add a bit of old-fashioned glamour, like these belonging to Sandy Gallin.

This huge bathroom belonging to Sandy Gallin is made more intimate with the warmth of a cozy rug and squishy slipcovered chair and footstool. The endless stacks of plush white towels give it a fresh, clean look.

ABOVE: The bathrooms in Sandy Gallin's Malibu home are filled with simple, beautiful containers made of wood, glass, and marble and hold an array of sundries. (CLOCKWISE FROM TOP LEFT) A marble dish holds creamy soaps; a glass fish bowl contains imported soaps in little boxes; a wooden box contains fine linen hand towels; glass jars in the guest bathroom hold bath crystals and oils .

OPPOSITE: When using pieces found at salvage yards or flea markets, such as the sink shown here, always take care to replace rusted parts and faulty piping with updated fixtures. No matter how great a piece looks, if it's meant to function, it should. Adding to the practicality of this simple, monochromatic bathroom, the wainscoting was painted with a high-gloss finish for easy maintenance.

LEFT: The practical and the aesthetic merge in this soothing green, light-filled Malibu bathroom. Since the bathroom had no built-ins, an old, peeling green cabinet is used for storing unattractive necessities.

TOP RIGHT: This decaying Victorian mantel, beads framing its beveled mirror, illustrates rich detail. That a small part of the curled design on the left of the mantel is broken does not detract from the beauty of the piece. Functionally, the mantel offers extra shelf space for perfumes, vases, and boxes.

BOTTOM RIGHT: A floral painting done on glass circumvents the damage steam can do to canvas. A wide window shelf and tile ledges around the bathtub provide ample space for soaps, flowers, a mirror, bath oils, and even a cup of tea.

ABOVE: Refined accents add an air of formality to a basic bathroom. A chandelier, gold-framed mirrors, white lace curtains, and Italian footstools are elegant touches in Philomena Giusti's otherwise simple white and wood master bath.

LEFT: A bouquet of silk flowers is an unexpected touch at the base of this Italian footstool in Giusti's master bath. Gold metal rope, tassels, and a leopard-print cushion add to the visual surprise.

OPPOSITE: Simplicity of color and wood unify Giusti's light and airy master bath. A black reproduction vintage bathtub with silver feet is updated with the addition of a wire rack that keeps soaps and oils well within reach. A fluffy white towel, a welcome element in any bathroom, hangs nearby, while an ornate gold-framed mirror enlarges the sense of space and reflects the colorful tile details of the shower.

EATING AREAS

Whether a dining room, a kitchen, or a table on a terrace, eating areas should be comfortable, enticing places where atmosphere and decor do not take precedence over function, but encourage socializing and make guests and residents alike feel at home. The basics of any eating area are a sturdy, functional (and preferably large) table with comfortable seating and soft lighting. Kitchens, with their aura of warmth, are a natural place for families and guests to gravitate toward. Since more and more families are eating and entertaining in the kitchen these days, it's ideal for this room to offer a roomy table and plenty of accommodating seating.

Table settings are what usually create the atmosphere for an eating area. My favorite table settings are mismatched in terms of dishes, chairs, napkins, and even silverware. Mismatched place settings render a formal setting less stiff and add whimsy. The mismatching can be as blatant as using completely different colors and patterns at every place setting, or as subtle as using different patterns in the same shade or two. (I like to use variations of Old Willow—a traditional English blue and white pattern.) The hodgepodge effect of using mismatched pieces can be achieved by either combining your own sets of dishes or by actually purchasing single pieces from various sets at flea markets and creating your own look (see Chapter 3, "Hidden Treasures and Inspirations"). Either way, there are no rules.

While tablecloths can be beautiful additions to tabletops, I sometimes dispense with them altogether and let the scratched character of the table show through. I also like the idea of using a formal dining room very casually, as Philomena Guisti does, mixing a twelve-dollar tablecloth with real silver, and using a casual setting like the outdoors in a formal way, with crystal glasses and linens.

Mismatched patterns add both charm and a casual air to table settings. At this table set for tea, I used blue and white to mirror the cool, peaceful hues of the sea outside the window, although no dish or fabric cushion at the table matches another precisely. A vintage lace curtain was thrown casually over the chipped green picnic table, and a fresh arrangement of flowers was placed at the end of the setting so as not to impair guests' views. (See Resource Guide.)

ABOVE: An old standing cabinet with chicken-wire sides finds a new function as a hanging cupboard for an array of towels, teacups, bowls, and mugs in the corner of Philomena Giusti's kitchen.

OPPOSITE: The intimate dining room of Giusti's Spanish-style home illustrates how the formal and the informal, and the expensive and the inexpensive, combine to achieve a pleasing effect. A grand feast or a light snack are equally suitable in this room, where a white lace drape found at a flea market serves as the tablecloth for a French country wine taster's table surrounded by well-worn leather-backed chairs. A simple bouquet of fresh roses from the garden placed casually in a silver vase and a pair of crystal candle-holders serve as a centerpiece, while an antique chandelier adds an air of faded grandeur.

ABOVE: The food itself can be an intregal part of a dining room's decor. These cucumber sandwiches, blueberries and cream, honeydew, apples, and grapes blend together and with the table setting to create a cool tranquillity. (See Resource Guide.)

OPPOSITE: This bright alcove off Tony and Donna Scott's kitchen is put to good use. A scratched and worn wooden table and benches are used for quick meals or snacks, as a temporary holding area for purses, keys, and magazines, and as a space to set a large, fresh bouquet from the garden. An iron chandelier painted green adds a soft glow, while in the corner an antique masthead from a ship's bow seems to watch over the room. "This room is really the heart of the house," says Donna of the kitchen area. "Guests always seem to end up congregating here because it feels so comfortable."

OPPOSITE: While subtle, muted tones are the usual markings of the Shabby Chic style, a mix of fabrics in a range of colors and patterns can make a tabletop more inviting, if not exciting. This Moroccan-style feast on Tony and Donna Scott's poolside terrace blends colorful foods with bright dishes and a rainbow of fabrics in differing Indian-print patterns to create an eclectic, tapestrylike atmosphere. (See Resource Guide.)

RIGHT: These etched blue glasses from France are a tiny size perfect for children, who never seem to finish the contents of a large glass. The glasses are inexpensive and come in an array of fun colors that can be mixed and matched with different fabric patterns. Here, they're paired with linen and lace placemats from my daughter Lily's doll tea set.

TIPS FOR TABLES

- ☐ If you're able to without creating too much clutter, have everything on the table you think you're going to need before the meal begins. It can be helpful and creates an abundant look. Otherwise, you'll be constantly getting up and down. This is also especially helpful if you have children, who always seem to be asking for something else.

- ☐ Centerpieces should be low or put at the end of the table. You want your guests to be able to see and talk to one another. It's also nice if the centerpiece carries out the colors or theme of the meal.

- ☐ Buffets are a great way to create a relaxed atmosphere and are an especially good choice when children will be among your guests. Children can be finicky eaters and buffets give them lots of choices.

- ☐ Candles are a must, for they set a wonderful mood and emanate flattering light both for food and people. It can be attractive to display all different shapes and sizes, but make sure there is adequate light. People should be able to see what they're eating.

- ☐ The bigger the table, the better—room permitting.

LIVING ROOMS

The most important quality of a living room is that it can actually be lived in. Rather than being a showpiece, a living room should be a functioning space for socializing, reading, and relaxing. Regardless of its style, a living room should maximize comfort with seating arranged in a way that is conducive to conversation.

Even very formal living rooms can be made to feel more casual. Furniture that wears well, like leather, which can actually improve with age, or slipcovered chairs, which remove the fear of stains, can make a formal living room more welcoming. The elimination of anything too precious and the belief that objects are to be used, not merely looked at, are other ways to keep a living room from becoming too stuffy. If something breaks, tears, or gets stained, this should not constitute a crisis. Pieces with wrinkles or imperfections further open the door toward real living. Candles that have been burned, throw blankets that are really used, and earmarked books are all signs of life that make a room more inviting.

Coffee tables should be roomy enough for books, magazines, resting feet, flowers, and tea cups. Personal objects such as framed family photographs add individuality, while mirrors are good for maximizing space in small living rooms. Mirrors should be hung where they will reflect light and something interesting—the view from a window can provide both.

Regarding fabrics and colors, I prefer muted tones, monochromatic color schemes, and subdued themes for living rooms as evidenced by the variations of pale greens, creams, and subtle floral patterns in my own house. But, as in any other room, unexpected touches and contrasts sometimes can be appealing additions (see Chapter 4, "Fabrics").

OPPOSITE: Chantall Cloutier's theatrical living room is a good illustration of how a white denim slipcover can work anywhere as a base for layering color. The throw is made from an old piece of floral fabric lined in velvet. The coffee table is a vintage door painted white and topped with a piece of glass. A marble plant pedestal, gilded mirror, candles, and oil paintings are touches that add a rich feel.

RIGHT: The white slipcovers
ease the formal mood of Sandy
Gallin's living room.
FOLLOWING PAGES: Tony and
Donna Scott's octagon-shaped
living room.

68

FORGOTTEN SPACES

Entryways, halls, foyers, staircases, and doorsteps are all "nonrooms" that have incredible potential to become interesting spaces, but they are all too often passed by on one's way to another space—in other words, ignored. Often these areas are the first things a visitor sees, so imbuing them with aesthetically appealing characteristics can serve to create a good first impression. Forgotten spaces are perfect spots for decorative pieces like chandeliers, paintings, intricate banisters, or colorful tiles—all of which give a house added character.

The little details that actress Jennifer Nicholson added to her front door area, for example, give visitors a glimpse of her personal taste and set a tone for the ambiance of her home. She hung a crystal chandelier on the doorstep, painted the door seafoam green, and added a sheet of etched glass behind the door's wrought-iron floral peephole. Upon opening the front door to Philomena Giusti's house, visitors are greeted by a colorful staircase with different tiles on every step. Tony and Donna Scott's front entryway could have been left as a mere passage, but the couple turned it into a functioning space with visual appeal instead. They installed a comfortable bench, added a mirror framed in peeling old architectural molding, and put in a traditional hat rack to allow for easy access to jackets. Hallways and staircase

LEFT: **In Sandy Gallin's high-tech black, chrome, and mirrored gym, the cushy, white slipcovered chairs and couch create a cozy contrast to the hard-edged workout equipment.**

OPPOSITE: **Entrances create one of the first impressions of one's home for visitors and as such should not be overlooked. This seafoam green door at Jennifer Nicholson's Spanish-style home demonstrates how an appreciation for detail can make a difference. Nicholson first had the door painted her favorite color, then installed a piece of etched glass behind the floral iron grating covering the peephole.**

LEFT: The elements within a room or even the parts of the same structure need not match to be appealing. To add color and detail to the front stairway of her home, Philomena Giusti covered each step with a different Malibu tile. "I wanted every step to be individual," she explains. "It gives an early California feel to the house, which is Spanish-style but could have gone in a French direction."

OPPOSITE: Front entryways with warmth and character, such as this sunny, earth-toned entrance at the home of film director Tony Scott and his wife, Donna, welcome visitors. Visual appeal and function come together in this well-used space, where the life of the home is evident. A built-in seating area covered in inviting leather, a traditional hat rack filled with jackets, and leather dog leashes strung over the banister offer evidence of the occupants' comings and goings. A Shabby Chic mirror, with its compos detailing and peeling and worn frame, serves as a spot for last-minute touch-ups. Cleaning footprints is easy on this cool tile floor.

landings throughout the Scotts' house are put to good use with desks that serve as junk holders; sunny, pillow-filled window seats for reading; glass tables for holding pretty floral arrangements; and a variety of decorative yet functional lighting fixtures.

Nontraditional rooms such as home offices and gyms are other areas that are often overlooked from a design standpoint. Chantall Cloutier's home office exemplifies how aesthetics and function can merge successfully. A fax machine, telephone, and date book blend in with vintage pieces Cloutier picked up at flea markets and antique shops. She uses an ornately carved wooden table as a desk, old fireplace andirons as bookends, and the surprise of an antique mirror over the desk to create a sense of space. Sandy Gallin's home gym is another example of how a nontraditional room can be made into a very decorative yet functional space. The enveloping white slipcovered sofas and chairs and a dark wooden table offer a respite from the room's hard-edged chrome and sleek equipment.

Whether a room is the bustling heart of a home or a private sanctuary, the best way to transform it into a comfortable, livable space is to let purpose take the lead and allow appearances or aesthetics to follow. It is also important to keep an open mind about new functions for old forms and to break away from outdated rules about formality and informality. The vintage bedroom vanity used as a bathroom cabinet, the rusty gate transformed into a coffee table, the chipped yet grand chandelier placed in the bathroom, the faded twelve-dollar tablecloth used in a formal dining room—these are the details that create the most interesting rooms and give them the character that is so important to the Shabby Chic style.

3

—

Hidden
Treasures &
Inspirations

A faded, peeling old dresser; a cracked white chandelier; a chipped, metal trash can painted with roses: To one person, these items are rejects for the junkyard, to another, they are a bounty of riches. Discovering beauty in and finding new uses for the old and worn discards of others greatly appeals to me, and there is no better place to find the faded and the decayed, the crumbling and the scuffed than a salvage yard or flea market, garage or estate sale.

Most cities and towns have salvage or junk yards, and most also offer some sort of market for secondhand items. Salvage yards are great for finding old bathroom fixtures or iron works, but tend to be a bit more expensive than flea markets, which usually reap the biggest and most economical crops of shabby pieces with the potential to evolve into chic treasures. Although flea markets vary from city to city, I find that weekly markets are less worthwhile than monthly markets, as a week isn't enough time for vendors to restock their inventory.

Articles I like to look for at swap meets include: tapestries and rugs with floral or romantic motifs; lamps (metal wall sconces from the forties are great); crystal or metal chandeliers (but nothing too gaudy); candleholders; floral paintings; vases; wicker furniture (preferably of a

PREVIOUS PAGES AND ABOVE: **New functions for old forms:** Found at a flea market, these attractive metal bowls were once the halves of globe-shaped street lamps. Some were lined with cloth, others with glass bowls from the local drugstore, while still others were left as is, depending on their contents. Here, the lamp pieces are used as whimsical holders for fruit, bread, eggs, and a candle, with a crisp piece of cotton and lace serving as a backdrop.

thick, sturdy variety); painted wood pieces, such as peeling vanities, dressers, and cabinets in pale colors or in colors that can be repainted; architectural moldings; iron-work furniture; and mirrors. (Don't be put off by slight mottling, which can give a mirror added character. Do be wary, though, of mottling that creates too much distortion, rendering the mirror no longer functional.)

I also look for pieces that have multiple uses or the potential for new uses, such as trunks, doors, or gates that can be used as coffee tables; or metal-work half-spheres that were once part of lamps that can be used as bowls for flower petals, candles, or fruit. Old wooden door or window moldings and iron works in intricate patterns and patinas can make great mirror frames. Good architectural moldings come from demolition sites of old houses and can be found at junk yards and some flea markets. I avoid moldings that

RIGHT: **The interesting shape and floral detailing on this chair made it stand out from the rest of its flea market stall-mates.**

BELOW RIGHT: **This flea market trunk was in great condition and would barely need any handling.**

BELOW: **Delicate and shabby, faded velvet roses on this vintage flea market find struck me as being quite beautiful.**

FOLLOWING PAGES: **A typical vendor stand is a mishmash of bits and bobs, odds and ends, clutter and clatter. Once your eye becomes trained, however, certain pieces will stand out as you learn to distinguish between trash and treasure.**

are too scraped up and have more wood showing than paint, because they look too "country" for my taste. I like just enough dilapidation to render character, not true decay.

Flea markets also can be ripe ground for unique pieces. If an object has no real purpose and is purely ornamental, I prefer that it exhibit unusual or whimsical characteristics that imbue it with humor or life. Parts of an object, for example, such as the foot, hand, or head of a statue, can be as beautiful as the whole.

For me, scouting flea markets is never about searching for objects with a certain value or status, that are from a specific period, or by a certain designer. Flea markets are where I find items that I am drawn to instinctively, due to their unique look, their workmanship, their feel, or their character. The attraction for a piece also might be that it seems simply perfect for that empty corner in the bedroom or that out-of-the-way space under the stairs.

FAR RIGHT: This humble wicker chair cost a friend twenty dollars at a flea market and an additional one hundred and fifty dollars to have a small frayed area on the arm repaired. The intricate detailing and the green paint peeking through the peeling white paint give the chair a mottled appearance that I find appealing, although the entire chair could easily be repainted white for a clean, fresh look. (See Resource Guide.)

BELOW: Old window and door moldings make great frames for pictures and mirrors. I look for those in muted colors with enough peeling and crumbling to lend texture but not so much that the piece looks as if it will fall apart. Salvage yards, flea markets, and demolition sites are good places to look for moldings.

To beat the crowds and to benefit from the widest choice, the most opportune time to go to a market or meet is when it first opens, usually around six A.M. I like to arrive at sunrise, when the vendors are still unloading their vans and trucks. Flea markets have become so popular in the last few years and competition for the best pieces so fierce that I try to snatch up pieces before they even make it off the truck.

Those with an eye on value, however, should consider a trip at the end of the day, which is a good time to get bargains from tired sellers, who, anxious to get rid of their wares, are more amenable to giving discounts.

It's also a good idea to get to know the market a little before buying. Stroll around to assess the variety of offerings and compare prices. Some sellers may even put items on hold for a few hours, enabling you to do a bit of comparison shopping without losing the object you're interested in. Take your time, especially if you are new to the world of flea markets. Once you become seasoned, you'll be able to sense immediately if something is "right" and if the asking price is reasonable. If you buy often enough and in quantity, you can build a relationship with certain vendors, who may even purchase items specifically with you in mind. When I wander around flea markets, sellers often point out some decrepit cabinet and tell me it reminded them of something they thought I'd like.

Don't be afraid to walk away from something. When I really like a piece, I try to act as nonchalant as possible, for if a seller can tell you're going to buy something, he has no incentive to give you a better price. If you appear hesitant, he may come down a few dollars to entice you. When I see someone else looking at an object that I like, I won't show that I'm interested when he puts the object down; I wait until that person actually leaves the stall. Many times a potential buyer has put something down only to become suddenly reinterested when I showed interest, too. Sensing a demand for an item can also make the seller ask a higher price. When the seller does name his price, you might want to offer anywhere from 20 to 40 percent less so that you can come to a compromise somewhere in between. It's better to barter with cash, and you can also expect better discounts if you buy in quantity.

If you're not buying an object immediately but want to remember where it is, or if you want to come back later to pick up a purchase, jot down the stall number where you found it. If there are no numbers, make note of the surroundings. I often write down little notes to myself like "mirror at stall next to big blue awning, near red truck."

Though a worn-out, weathered look is a quality I look for, it makes sense to look for things that aren't too damaged, especially if you don't have a lot of time and money for restoration. There is sometimes a fine line between trash and treasure, and only the buyer can decide when junk really is just junk. If a piece needs a major restructuring job, is extremely delicate, or if repainting will ruin it or make it look too fake, it might not be worth buying. Trying to restore wicker that is too dilapidated can be as frustrating as attempting to repair a run in a stocking, not to mention expensive. If the flaw is something simple like a torn piece on the seating, I just add a pillow. If the imperfection is a tiny bit of tattered arm, I might decide to live with it. I have a friend who bought an old paper-wrapped wicker rocker for twenty dollars and spent a hundred and fifty dollars to restore it. For her, the piece was so beautiful and rare, restoring it was worth the expense.

OPPOSITE: This old painted dresser was in great shape, with interesting details—I painted it cream.

RIGHT: Before: I loved the muted sea-green color of this old painted headboard. Rather than repaint it, I left the piece peeling and crumbling, and later turned it into a daybed topped with a patchwork of pink floral and cream bedspreads and pillows.

FOLLOWING PAGES: After: To transform this headboard and frame, I added big fabric bolsters to the back and sides. For a casual feel, I used a mixture of plaids, florals, and solids and covered the mattress with an Indian-print bedspread of the type that can be purchased at import stores for fifteen or twenty dollars. All I did to the dresser was add some green glass knobs. To make the Roman blinds, I used inexpensive bedcovers and kept them unlined for a natural, sun-bleached feel.

The fruits of a two-hour stop at the flea market. I picked up about twenty-six items on this particular morning, including everything from dressers and trunks to lamp shades and metal baskets.

Equally as important as avoiding pieces that are too worn is avoiding overly perfect or faux old pieces, like furniture that has been painted or repainted, then intentionally scraped and scratched to look worn. With the increasing popularity of vintage painted wooden furniture, this faux old phenomenon is becoming more common as truly authentic vintage pieces become more scarce. To discern if something is truly old versus merely made to appear that way, look for defects that are more random than uniform and colorations that are varied or appear in gradations. Paint jobs that look stroked on only in patches or deliberately rubbed away in spots are other signs of fake aging. To buy a piece that you will have to turn into something shabby is to miss the point, for the appeal of a piece is in its natural aging, not in the false creation of the appearance of age. If I feel as if I would need to chip away at a piece with a hammer or scrape it with sandpaper to give it an aged feel, I forgo it. In addition to distinguishing between real old versus fake old, hunt for pieces that are substantial and have some weight to them—in other words, that aren't too fragile or rickety—and articles with evidence of craftsmanship.

Objects with a real history and a defect or two are more appealing and somehow more approachable, so don't be put off by a few places where the oak wood peeks through a pale green vanity table or by rusty patches of metal on an old candleholder. The beauty is in the imperfection. The charm is in the flaw.

Details give objects an added aesthetic appeal and make the difference between the ordinary and the unique collector's piece. An intricate floral wreath on the drawer of a tiny, chipped green dresser was the selling point that made me take notice. A screen underneath, once used to keep bugs out, gave the piece a historical dimension, and the fact that it was held together by interlocking pieces of wood rather than nails authenticated its age. Carved or painted flower motifs always add to the value of a piece. Because labor costs are so prohibitive, it's rare to find in new furniture a flower carving that is not a separate, decorative piece that was attached later. While these attached pieces can be quite lovely, and I have used them on occasion to dress up the edges of mirrors, authentic carvings are preferable.

The legs and edges of a vanity, end table, or chair are also good indicators of quality and age. Most vanities made between the turn of the century and the forties have fluted rather than straight-edged surfaces, and their legs tend to be curved and detailed. Curved or bowed drawers are other desirable and hard-to-find features.

In iron works, be they lighting fixtures, gates, frames, tables, or chairs, I look for fine detailing and steer away from pieces that are too clunky or crude. In a toile floral chandelier, for example, I examine the flowers for their intricacy and realism, for the delicacy of their edges and curves, and for the fineness of their lines. Iron works from the forties and earlier are usually more detailed than later works. Because iron works often come in black, I almost always paint them ivory.

RIGHT: The intricate flower carvings and architectural patterns on this vintage dresser are evidence of its age and give it aesthetic appeal.

FOLLOWING PAGES:

(PAGE 90) The fine workmanship and well-thought-out proportions are what attracted me to this turn-of-the-century blue Italian bedside table. Its tapered shape, floral detail, and casters are all features that add to its character and reveal its authenticity.

(PAGE 91) This nineteenth-century French bedside table is a fine example of what to look for in vintage pieces, as it exhibits incredible detail and has an almost sensuous quality owing to its curved legs, drawers, and sides and the intricately painted flowers on its front and sides. The faded color of the paint and the various crackles add to the piece's time-worn appeal.

CLEANING AND REPAIRING

Easy ways to spruce up objects that need only minimal help include painting, adding new hardware or lining, or placing a piece of fabric, marble, or glass over a problem area.

If a table, cabinet, or wicker rocker, for example, is attractive in shape and proportion, but is stained in an ugly brown or lime green, it can find new life with a coat of white or cream paint. Semigloss or gloss paint is best, as a matte finish tends to absorb too much dirt. I will give wood pieces a light scour with a bristle brush or sponge and some soap and warm water. (Once the dirt is removed, if

the look and texture still aren't right, the piece can be very lightly sanded—but only lightly; a strenuous sanding can ruin a piece's weathered look. If the piece has been painted with gloss paint, it may need to be sanded a little more.) Then I prime and paint the piece. If I'm going to repaint a piece that has painted hardware, and the piece is already a color I like, I'll leave the hardware as is in order to keep some of its original shabbiness intact. I simply cover the hardware with tape while I paint the rest. The end result is a freshly painted piece with crackled, peeling hinges or handles. Because wicker is so fragile, I don't recommend sanding it or washing it too roughly. Wicker is also fairly absorbent, so I prefer to paint it as is so that it retains some of its coarse texture.

Revamping a piece of vintage furniture can be as easy as replacing unsightly knobs and handles or adding old casters.

ABOVE LEFT: This pile of antique casters includes wood, brass, steel, porcelain, and rubber rollers from the seventeenth through the twentieth centuries. In the late 1800s and early 1900s it was not uncommon for dining room tables, dressers, and kitchen cabinets to have casters for easy mobility. (See Resource Guide.)

LEFT: These glass, crystal, and porcelain knobs date from the late eighteenth through twentieth centuries. (See Resource Guide.)

OPPOSITE: Older knobs and handles with more character can be found at vintage hardware stores such as Liz's Antique Hardware in Los Angeles. They can also be discovered at some salvage yards, or can be scavenged from other pieces of furniture. (See Resource Guide.)

If the knobs or handles on a vanity are too new or unattractive, or if they are missing, they easily can be replaced with detailed antique porcelain, glass, or crystal fixtures. Ranging in price from about seven to forty dollars per knob at vintage hardware outlets (they may run slightly cheaper at salvage yards or flea markets but are harder to find), antique fixtures are not a bargain. But they are well worth the expenditure, as they add to the quality and interest of a piece. The pieces needn't match, either. If you keep an underlying theme—all glass knobs of the same size but with different designs etched on them, for example—the effect can be even more charming than a perfectly matched set.

When the top of a dresser is beyond repair, marred by too many scratches or worn out pieces of wood, I might cover it with a piece of vintage lace then top the lace with a sheet of glass (glass costs an average of fifteen to twenty dollars per square foot—slightly more if the glass has beveled edges). I may also conceal the damaged area with a slab of marble, which I often use to rejuvenate the tops of consoles or side tables. I opt for dull rather than shiny, glitzy finishes and for marble that is gray, white, or cream with gray or brown veins, as these colors are more versatile, working well in a variety of surroundings. Marble from a marble and/or glass specialist can run anywhere from about seven to one hundred dollars

per square foot, or more, depending on its quality, color, and thickness; the marble dealer I use has more than one hundred different styles to choose from. The edging treatment of the marble can also add to its cost. A three-by-three-foot slab of a basic marble with rounded rather than flat edges costs anywhere from $250 to $325. Where appropriate, I prefer rounded, bull-nosed edges; these cost a little more but create a facade of extra thickness.

Though wicker furniture is fairly hardy despite its frail appearance, weatherproofing is a good idea if the furniture will be exposed to the ravages of sun and rain for an extended period of time. Adding a coat of paint is one way to lengthen the life of wicker (LEFT); another way is to cover it with a sheet of glass (OPPOSITE).

I use pieces in ways that are different from their original intention. This pale yellow antique vanity retrieved from a flea market (LEFT) was later placed in a bathroom lacking built-ins, where it functions as a cabinet for towels, toiletries, and other bathroom necessities (ABOVE). The mirror is useful, while the top of the vanity serves as a place for a pretty lace runner, a brush and comb set, and family photographs.

This old green chest of office drawers I picked up at a flea market (RIGHT) works perfectly as a storage space for paints, fabrics, and other odds and ends in this light-filled artist's studio (BELOW). Finding its degree of shabbiness perfect, all I did to restore the cabinet was to add some new glass knobs.

For iron table bases that lack lipped edges to set the glass or marble into, I buy glass or marble that is approximately two to six inches bigger all the way around in order to create a slight overhang. To keep the glass or marble from slipping, I secure it with small pieces of green felt that can be purchased at hardware stores for just this purpose. With small end tables, I might replace the glass with a cushion to create a small seat.

Mirror, like glass, is not expensive—a plain four-by-four-foot mirror costs around forty dollars, but runs about a dollar per inch more if it has beveled edges. The type of mirror I choose depends on how intricate the frame is. For a very detailed wrought-iron floral frame, I would probably use plain mirror. For a simple wooden frame, beveled mirror adds nice detail. Whatever frame you use, make sure the mirror is securely fastened. This is best achieved with wood bracing.

For old cabinets, I either repaint the inside, add contact paper, or put in a mirrored back to give the illusion of depth. If the inside back isn't too decrepit, I may leave it as is to keep some of its character.

A trunk with an inside that is a bit dilapidated can be inexpensively freshened up with a fabric lining and a satchel of potpourri. Be sure to check the trunk for termites before lining it. (Termites can be easily gotten rid of with a spray treatment.) For an average-size trunk, you'll need anywhere from a half to two or three yards of fabric, the price of which can vary enormously in price per yard, depending on the material and its quality. You might even use some old fabric scraps from around the house. I usually use an inexpensive cotton floral that I

I placed a slab of marble atop this somewhat rickety, weathered iron console to give it substance as well as ground it. The mercury glass vases are from the turn of the century. A few years ago they could be bought for about fifty dollars apiece; now they have become so popular that they may sell for as much as three hundred to four hundred dollars each.

If a tapestry is too worn, with large rips in prominent places, or just looks too delicate, I walk away from it no matter how lovely it is, because it will very likely fall apart. However, if, like this tapestry I picked up at a flea market (LEFT), it is merely frayed in spots, it may be well worth the restoration. Loose threads can be fixed by catching them with another thread about every one half inch or so as needed (INSET). In more extreme cases, edges and hems can be cut and new pieces of fabric added as trimming and rein-forcement.

simply tack on with push pins, although fabric also can be fastened in place with a staple gun or fabric glue.

Tapestries with frayed edges can be refurbished by catching stray threads and/or cutting off the damaged area and adding a new fabric border that acts as a reinforcement. If the fabric is too moth-eaten, avoid it, as it will eventually deteriorate.

Overall, when shopping a flea market, I look for items that have character but aren't completely dilapidated. The less one has to fuss with an object, the better. Not only does a minimum of tampering better maintain the original integrity of an item, but it also means a lot less work for the buyer. There are, however, times when there is something so unique or eye-catching about a piece that it can't be passed up, no matter how involved the restoration process.

WHAT TO BRING TO A FLEA MARKET

- ☐ A flashlight: A crack that may look charming in the darkness of dawn may be a disaster by the light of noon. Be sure you can see what you're getting.
- ☐ Cash: Having plenty of cash on hand is more likely to get you good deals and some vendors don't accept checks.
- ☐ A cart or dolly: Lugging pieces back and forth to your vehicle can get very tiring with-out a cart or dolly, and some pieces are just too heavy to be carried on their own. Some vendors may be willing to lend you their carts, but others won't.
- ☐ A truck: Borrow one from a friend or rent one for the day if you're planning to buy large or numerous pieces. There's nothing more frustrating than having inadequate room to carry your purchases home. Very few vendors will deliver.
- ☐ Cords, rope, and blankets: Bring plenty of rope and bungee cords to insure a secure transport home. Blankets help protect pieces of furniture from damage and breakage. It's especially important to wrap mirrors, glass, and wicker.
- ☐ Fingerless gloves: These keep your hands warm while still allowing for maneuverabil-ity. Bulky gloves might make you hesitate about touching or picking up objects, which is a big part of choosing a piece.

INSPIRATIONS

There is a lot more to creating a beautiful, functional living space than skimming through lifestyle magazines, reading design books, and consulting interior decorators. Plays, movies, life events, articles of clothing, or accessories may also provide inspiration for home design as well as new uses for old forms and ideas for unexpected placement of new forms. A circus might reap a color idea or salvage parts perfect for a child's room. The petticoat from a theater costume spurred me to create a new ruffle to be used for a tablecloth and napkins. A wreath design on a vintage sewing bag I picked up was the inspiration for a new fabric pattern.

Observing people and animals and how they sit, snuggle, move, and interact can influence the design of a piece of furniture or its placement in a room. I created a round, low, cushy fabric chair I call the Pouf after watching my daughter, Lily, and son, Jake, and their friends consistently choose to plop on the floor rather than the couch, complaining all the while about how uncomfortable it was as they lolled about—an example of necessity truly being the mother of invention or of function serving as inspiration.

For me, the landscape is a great place to find stimulation for design. Flowers or seashells, for example, often can be used in new and unexpected ways. I've used roses and other flowers to adorn cakes, deco-

ABOVE: I call this oversized fabric poster "The Lonely Clown." Cut from a big-top tent canvas, this was the remaining loner unsold for several months after I had sold thirty-eight others in sets of two. But eventually it too found a home. Pieces like this are the perfect impetus for decorating an entire children's room.

RIGHT: Although I usually prefer mismatched table linens, I found these gossamer napkins of iridescent gold organza belonging to Jennifer Nicholson inspiring. Their holders made from seashells also have an appealing elegance.

rate mirrors and presents, and accompany place settings. The random color variations in a meadow or field and the scale and proportions of those variations can inspire color schemes. Observing the subtle gradations of greens and creams in a garden, I used those same hues in the design of sofa and chair fabrics. Looking to nature's imperfections and the natural wear and tear that occurs over time induces a new appreciation for flaws and irregularities in manmade objects. The faded, dusty pink of a dying rose has inspired me to sun-bleach a bright floral fabric over time in order to mimic a real rose's natural passage from vivid to muted.

Personal collections, whether family photographs or something as commonplace as children's art, can inspire a display that gives a home individuality and character that cannot be acquired through a decor shop. I have strung some of my children's paintings across a clothes line and hung it above the counter in my kitchen. Others I have framed and hung in my bedroom.

When it comes time to finding a place in the home for flea market or other finds, I usually adhere to my less is more philosophy: negative space serves as my guide. Leaving ample breathing space around

large objects such as vanities and dressers gives a room a more open feel and prevents the jumbled look of clutter upon clutter, even if their surfaces are filled with personal treasures.

I also find inspiration from taking what is meant to be formal and placing it in a more casual setting. While giving the pleasing effect of making the object seem more accessible, this also renders the setting slightly more refined. A crystal chandelier, expected in a formal dining room or a grand entryway, is a

LEFT: A weathered, red wooden milk bucket, its surface scratched, its paint peeling from years of wear and tear, becomes a handy container for all kinds of utensils when placed on an iron plant holder in Philomena Giusti's kitchen.

OPPOSITE: Though often overlooked when decorating, wastepaper baskets can be attractive additions to a room. To make this wire-mesh basket more functional, I lined it with muslin to prevent small objects from slipping through. The wicker ones are appealing in their frayed state.

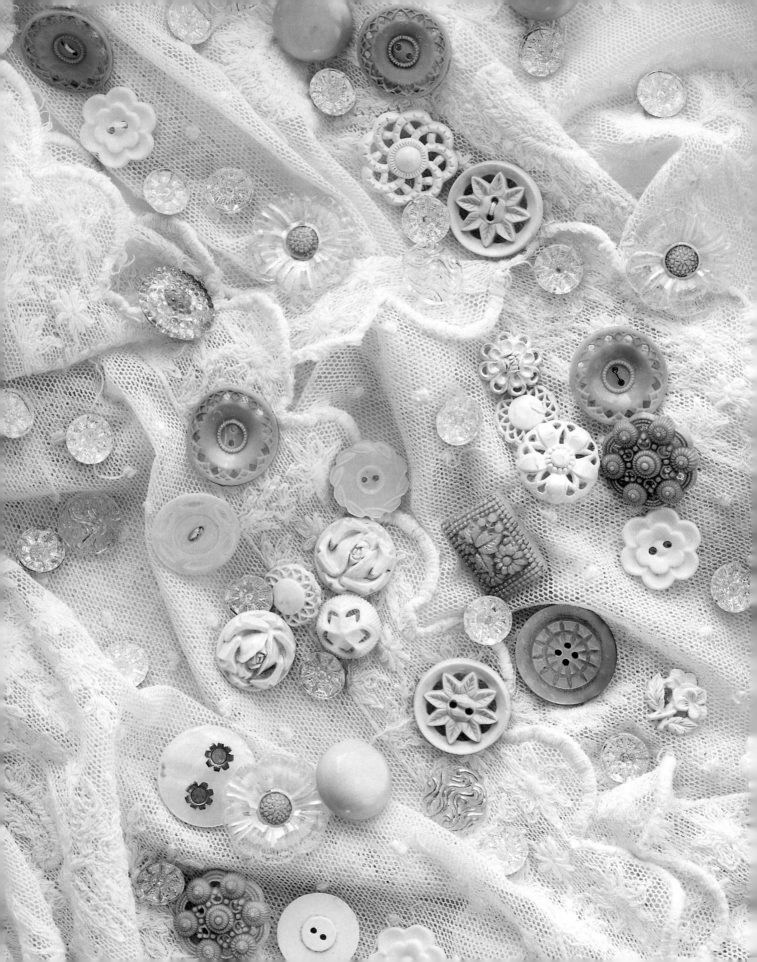

OPPOSITE: I add vintage buttons to the backs of pillows to give them additional visual interest and detail. I gravitate toward buttons with intricate patterns in glass, plastic, or tortoiseshell. These generally cost about one to five dollars at flea markets.

RIGHT: Photographs of family and friends are among our most personal articles, adding individuality to any room in a home. This collection of old and new portraits in Philomena Giusti's living room inspired her to display them within an attractive array of wood, silver, and enamel antique frames.

wonderful surprise in a bathroom, while a mirror designed for a fireplace mantle can give a hallway an air of casual grandeur. Taking the casual and placing it in a more formal setting, on the other hand, also sets up an appealing contrast. Metal patio furniture doesn't have to be relegated to the outdoors. An intricate iron-work garden table and chair set can be charming in a breakfast nook, study, or bedroom.

Inspiration is about paying attention to the smallest of details and noticing subtleties of form and color. Beauty is found not only in a finished object but in all its parts, the processes that create it, the evolution that transforms it, and the environment around it.

4
—
FABRICS

abrics are meant to be comfortable and inviting. Whether they are used to cover sofas and make them more plush, to prevent tables—and laps—from becoming stained by meals, to give layers of warmth to a bed, or to keep out—or let in—light from a window, fabrics serve a purpose. Fabrics also give visual life and depth to an environment.

Fabrics, more than any other decorative aspect of a room, are most influential in creating its overall ambiance. From couch to window, from bed to table, fabrics should lend softness, warmth, and color. Transforming bare landscapes into rich woven tapestries of texture, hue, and pattern, fabrics set tones of casual ease or grand formality. Draped or folded, stiff or falling gently, textiles lend flexibility and versatility to environments made of less mutable elements like glass, wood, stone, and metal. The main point to keep in mind is that fabrics should always be of fine quality. Good-quality fabrics last longer and wear better over time; this is why vintage fabrics of good quality are still so appealing.

The types of fabrics that are in keeping with a shabby yet chic mood are generally casual, light, loose, and flowing, rather than formal, dark, and stiff. I find that simple materials—a plain white muslin window shade, a washable cream denim slipcover, or a faded rose-print cotton tablecloth or pillow—work in a wide range of environments. Weight is another consideration. I use lighter fabrics such as cotton and linen to create a more casual or summery mood, and heavier velvets, damasks, and chenilles to create a formal or warm wintry feel.

Like a painted dresser that has naturally peeled over time or a wrought-iron table rife with rusty scratches, fabrics that have aged naturally, faded, been mended, and that are slightly rumpled are representative of Shabby Chic style. A

PREVIOUS PAGES: **The delicate, faded pattern on this vintage sewing bag inspired me to design a fabric that mimics its design.**

OPPOSITE: **This intricately layered tablecloth ruffle gathered up with three silk roses to display the lace cloth underneath was inspired by a petticoat costume from a theater production** (SEE SKETCH ABOVE). **While this particular cloth has its own series of ruffles, any tablecloth can be given this layered effect by putting a piece of lace underneath the cloth and gathering up a portion of it with some faux silk, cotton, or velvet flowers.**

couch with patches where the fabric has been worn by time or a faded tablecloth, its colors muted by long hours in the garden sunshine, offer traces of real living. If a spot on the back of a velvet chair gets too worn, I might drape it with a chenille, velvet, or cotton throw rather than replace the whole piece. Not only is this more economical, it adds a layer of texture and color that can be very inviting.

But while some stains can be ignored, covered up, or patched over, sometimes it's better to remove them altogether. If you're dealing with a white fabric and the treatments listed below don't work, you can try bleaching it, but experiment with a small spot before doing the whole piece. The key to removing a stain successfully is to act immediately—before the stain dries. Dried stains are far more tenacious than wet ones. When using professional stain removers, which are often inflammable, make sure you do so in an adequately vented area, carefully following label instructions.

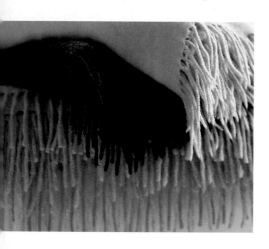

LEFT: Cashmere throws, the ultimate in luxury, can be used almost anywhere in the house, on beds, over chairs, or across the back of sofas. They add warmth, cover up imperfections, and can add new colors to a room's decor.

RIGHT: The white slipcovers in Sandy Gallin's living room are both durable and elegant.

FOLLOWING PAGES: These pillows show a variety of different ruffle and trim treatments.

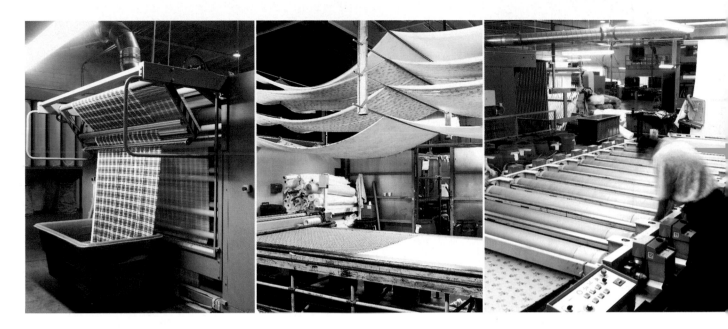

OPPOSITE: **These pots of paint illustrate the rainbow of color choices available today for fabrics.**

ABOVE LEFT: **For a brushed and softer feel, fabric is run through a sanding machine, like the one at this fabric factory.**

ABOVE CENTER: **Awaiting approval, samples of printed cotton fabric hang above a cutting table at a fabric factory. Five to ten yards are printed initially to make sure the color and registration are correct before running a major production.**

ABOVE RIGHT: **Here, rotary rollers imprint fabric. This process is less expensive than hand-screened printing and creates sharper definitions in pattern lines.**

When deciding between fabrics it's helpful to know that the variance between the processes and level of workmanship that go into creating different types of fabric patterns makes a marked difference in quality and price. The type of cloth used, the number of colors involved, whether a pattern is woven or printed, and the particular printing technique used are all factors in quality and price. A silk-screened linen fabric with several colors can cost up to a hundred dollars per yard, while a rotary-printed cotton with only two colors averages about twelve dollars per yard.

Whereas woven patterns are actually different colors of thread woven together into a design, printed fabrics are created by applying colors in certain forms to the surface of a fabric. Rotary, or machine, printing is by far the most common method used today. Metal rollers with tiny pinholes, engravings, or etched surfaces (also called intaglio) for different colors are rolled onto the fabric to create intricate, sophisticated patterns with clearly defined lines and subtleties of shading. Silk screening can be done either by hand or by machine, and is a variation of stenciling. A separate screen (or roller with mesh screens set into it) is used for each color for a specific design repetition. When one color dries, a new screen and color are added. Silk screening by hand gives a slight irregularity to a pattern and produces less defined forms. Like hand blocking, this imperfection adds character and individuality.

Hand blocking, the most primitive form of fabric printing, is done with actual blocks of wood with raised areas for color that get stamped onto a material. The resulting patterns, such as those found on Indian-print bedspreads and children's school projects, are imperfect yet quite charming and work very well when the idea is to create an informal, almost arts and crafts appearance for a particular room or table setting.

When I design fabrics, I usually let the base cloth determine my choice of silk-screened versus rotary-printed techniques. With linen, which is rougher than cotton, I most often use silk screening, which has a less defined look. For cotton, which has a smoother surface, the finer details of rotary printing work well.

In choosing a fabric for a particular room or piece of furniture, let both the function of the piece and the surroundings dictate your selection. Cotton is a more practical choice than linen for pieces that will suffer more wear and tear and undergo frequent laundering, as linen tends to shrink with every washing and is somewhat less sturdy.

When combining fabrics to come up with your own individual look, I recommend staying with fabrics that complement each other. I choose a common theme—either color, pattern, or texture—that will unite my different fabric choices and create the most harmonious look. Various shades of whites, creams, and beiges could be an underlying theme that appears in an array of textures, such as fine poplin, denim, damask, or nubby chenille—with or without patterns. A specific design—be it florals, stripes, or checks—could be an underlying theme that is repeated in a few or in a range of sizes and colors. Unexpected pairings and stark contrasts can also work if they are not overdone. The surprise of bright red pillows on a white bed or florals mixed with gingham can add life and whimsy to an otherwise predictable room.

Before buying a fabric, take a few swatches home with you. This way, you can judge whether the color looks different in the light of your home and whether it matches its potential surroundings. You might even want to buy a larger piece of fabric so you can experiment with the way it drapes as well as see more clearly how its pattern looks on a larger scale. If you choose silk-screened fabric, note that the inconsistency of dye lots from batch to batch may make it difficult for you to reorder the fabric in the exact color that you first purchased. That's why it's a good idea to buy extra yardage if you think you might need more of the fabric later. Then again, a perfect match may not be so important to you. Also, the farther away in the room an additional piece is from the original, the less noticeable the match.

These fabrics, which can be used for curtains, tablecloths, or upholstery, are among some of my favorites. (TOP TO BOTTOM) A classic red-striped cotton, a celadon stripe on a tea-stained linen, donkey plaid linen.

TOP: This willow damask becomes more puckered and dimensional with each washing.

ABOVE: A green rose and ribbon damask. Washing gives it a deeper texture.

RIGHT: This "blue grapes on oyster" print is hand silk-screened on linen.

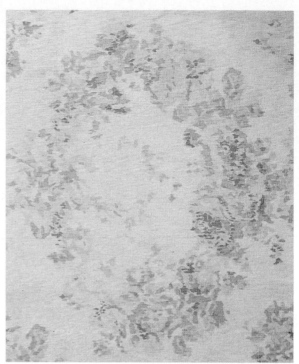

If you find a piece of vintage fabric that you want to turn into a bedspread, tablecloth, or curtain, but don't have enough material, consider adding a border or edge in a complementary fabric. Flea markets, textile specialists, and secondhand shops can be great resources for old lace and linen swatches as well as for Marseilles bedcovers in white-on-white cotton. (If the edges of Marseilles bedcovers are frayed, simply cut them off. Another alternative is to buy several different pieces and sew them together to create the size fabric you want.)

Don't be deterred by the rust stains very commonly found on lace, as they can usually be removed by over-the-counter stain products designed especially for this purpose. If the lace is

not too delicate, it can sometimes be bleached. A combination of crisp white cotton with lace trim looks beautiful and is usually easier to care for than an all-lace piece. This cotton and lace combination is also versatile; it can be laid on a tray, used as a guest towel, or placed in a bread basket as a liner.

Remember, you don't have to use a piece of fabric for its original purpose. A hardy lace curtain can make a great tablecloth and, conversely, an old lace tablecloth can make a pretty curtain.

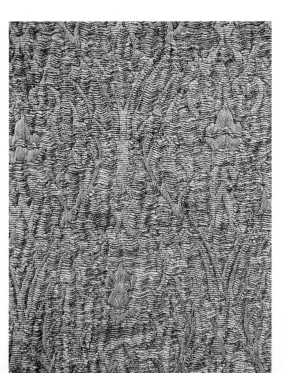

OPPOSITE: **Hand silk-screened on Belgian linen. (See Resource Guide.)**

LEFT: **An earth-green chenille. When washed, its colors become more defined, and the fabric more dimensional.**

ABOVE: **A new gray and white rose print on cotton chintz and its sun-bleached version, which appears naturally faded and feels softer.**

LEFT: This faded floral is an example of a hand-blocked cotton print that has become soft and muted due to repeat washings and exposure to sunlight. CENTER: A one-screen, hand-silk-screened print on linen. RIGHT: A one-screen rotary print on poplin.

WINDOW DRESSING

The function of a window covering, be it a curtain, drape, or blind, is to provide privacy and to keep out (or let in) light, heat, or cold. But as the French discovered in the late nineteenth century, curtains are also a great way to frame a window grandly and add decoration to a room. In intricate patterns and rich fabrics, with the addition of accessories such as pelmuts and valances shaped into swags, pleats, or rosettes, and using fancy trims such as banded ties, tassels, and ropes, curtains can become works of art.

I prefer window coverings made of fabrics that are simple and relaxed rather than fussy, soft rather than stiff, and shaped into loose rather than tight formations. I also prefer floaty gatherings, with a rounded rather than hard-edged look. In general, such arrangements are more casual than formal. Sometimes, though, I like to make the formal look more casual by using light easy-care fabrics. Lightweight velvets, moirés, muslins, and poplins are good for creating a floppy, draping effect, while tapestries, denims, damasks, and heavy velvets work to create a more structured mood. Like slipcovers, however, these more formal fabrics can be laundered to alleviate their severity.

For an unstructured, effortless look, windows should be draped with generous amounts of loose fabric that is allowed to puddle softly onto the floor. The simplicity of a plain white blind, such as the one covering the

LEFT: The handmade Scottish lace curtains in Jennifer Nicholson's dining room admit light yet still provide privacy.

ABOVE: This slightly transparent Roman shade with a delicate rose print adds a decorative touch to Tony and Donna Scott's guest house, yet still lets in plenty of natural light.

OPPOSITE: Jennifer Nicholson created a curtain out of an old cream lace bedspread depicting peasants gathering wheat. Accented by a vintage crystal chandelier, toile sconces, and a leopard print–covered stool, the entire entryway has vestiges of decadent glamour.

OPPOSITE: A simple Roman shade in a rose print adds life to this bathroom window in Tony and Donna Scott's home. Down, the shade is a decorative covering; up, it lets in sunlight and serves as a valance to frame the rectangular window.

ABOVE: This tapestry swag valance with a sheer underlining is an example of draped, flowing, loose window treatments. Though they add formality to a room, the curtains appear almost lazily hung, which makes them more approachable than stiffer, straight-lined drapery. (See Resource Guide.)

ocean view window in the living room of my beach house, works nicely, as do Roman shades, which give the appearance of a valance when pulled up, and balloon shades, which fold in soft billows.

Lining is an important element for helping curtains last longer and protecting them from the sun. Blackout lining—a dark fabric sandwiched between two pieces of white material—is good for bedrooms with eastern exposure that receive intense morning light. Thermaline lining helps insulate a room. Sheer underlinings made of chiffon, cheese-cloth, or batiste can be left closed all day to add privacy to a room while still letting in the light.

Above all, never skimp on yardage when choosing fabrics. Inadequate width or length can detract from the elegance and luxury of a dressed window.

L I N E N S

Bed linens are, above all, meant to provide luxury, warmth, and simple comfort, for these are the first fabrics to touch the skin in the morning and the last materials to do so at night. Because they are in such close contact with our bodies, natural fabrics, such as cotton, linen, and flannel, work best for sheets and blankets. Duvet covers or bedspreads, however, can be of richer velvets or silks.

Layering is key to the look and feel of a bed. Whether done in contrasting or complementary patterns and colors, layering gives a bed a pleasing visual and tactile impact, and offers a practical option of warmth should the night become cooler. Fabric pillows add color and depth. Overall, because beds serve as a sanctuary at the end of the day, their feel should be rich and inviting.

Whereas bedding is foremost about comfort, fabrics for the table are meant to protect the tabletop from the ritual scratches of silverware, the banging of dishes, the telltale rings of glasses, and the stains of daily feasts. Since table linens serve as the backdrop for entertaining and socializing, however, it is also desirable for them to be aesthetically pleasing. Whether you use an embroidered white linen covering or

a colorful chintz is a choice that depends upon whether a meal is formal or casual, though my preference, no matter the occasion, is a mix of the two.

My favorite table settings consist of mismatched fabrics (see Chapter 2, "Rooms"). If you have several incomplete sets of napkins, don't throw them out. Mix and match them in different colors and patterns, and use them with different tablecloths. I often see oddball sets of napkins at flea markets, where it's not unusual for vendors to sell them in threes or sevens. Like fabrics elsewhere in the home, table linens can boast a few wrinkles, exhibit some fading, expose frayed edges, and reveal a patch or two. The marks of time and years of enjoyment make them all the more appealing.

LEFT & TOP: **Beige poplin bedcover, pillows (see Resource Guide), and duvet.**
OPPOSITE: **In bedding, comfort is essential. I was inspired by the inviting feel of a baggy old T-shirt softened by years of use and washing for the soft, white, wrinkled sheets, pillowcases, and duvet cover on this old-fashioned iron bed.**

5
—
SEATING

Because sofas and chairs are the most important functional pieces in most of our living spaces, I want to give them special attention in this book. Although slipcovers are my first choice for chairs and sofas, leather and wicker are also materials that work well to create the Shabby Chic look. Leather is appealing because it is timeless, classic, natural, comfortable, and ages beautifully. I love wicker because it is lightweight, can be used indoors or outdoors, comes in an array of weaves, and can add an aura of casualness to otherwise formal surroundings.

If a leather piece is simply too worn, with distracting bare patches or scratches, parts of it can be reupholstered inexpensively without ruining the antique look of the whole. A different fabric can even be brought in to save money. I have replaced the worn leather cushion of an armchair with a velvet one, which added a new texture, cut down on cost, yet kept the piece plush. Wicker, though it can be costly to restore, is easy to repaint and has the uncanny ability to fit into a variety of different environments. (For more on wicker, see Chapter 3, "Hidden Treasures and Inspirations.")

When considering both the appeal and function of sofas and chairs, shape, size, and fabrics, and the way the pieces are placed in a room are all important elements. A chair meant for reading should be comfortable but not so cushy that it induces sleep, and it should of course be placed near good lighting. A chair for dining or the home office should be upright to facilitate eating or studying. Chairs meant for socializing should be comfortable and arranged in a way that promotes communication by minimizing the need to crane one's neck or raise one's voice to be heard. Seating meant for relaxing and napping, such as body pillows, poufs, chaises, and some armchairs, should be cushy, comfortable, soft, and over-sized—my favorite look. All these points may seem obvious, but it's amazing how many stiff, upright chairs I've seen that were intended by their owners to be comfortable and inviting.

PREVIOUS PAGES: Wicker—especially painted white—has long been a favorite material for outdoor furniture, due to its loose weave and easy portability. On Tony and Donna Scott's patio is an old convent bench that appears to be comprised of seven chairs fastened together. Its unusual length and comfortable striped cushion make it the perfect spot for a lazy afternoon nap for people and dogs alike. The cool stone walls and bougainvillea overhead add to the shady mood.

OPPOSITE: This worn leather chair in Philomena Giusti's home is marked by years of loving use. The faded patches and scratched studs make the chair an inviting sanctuary for one to curl up in and read. The original cushion, which became too tattered, was replaced with a velvet one. A silk pillow adds extra color and comfort.

Simply expanding the dimensions of a chair can give it a whole new function, like this extra-roomy slipcovered chaise. (See Resource Guide.)

In the case of sofas and chairs, need should dictate form. My children have inspired many of the chairs I've designed. An upholstered rocking chair was born after observing their love of rhythmic movement (although I installed a long wicker bench that resists rocking on one side of my dining room table, as the temptation for a child to rock while eating is just too great). I have also made arms on certain chairs rounder or bigger, backs straighter or more relaxed, depending on the intended use for a particular chair. Personal tastes can account for fabric choice, though for seating I suggest casual fabrics that can stand up to wear.

Ottomans or footstools not only elongate a chair by adding foot room, they also offer additional, casual seating in their own right and can add new colors, textures, and patterns to a room. Pillows are another way of bringing in color, detailing, and comfort to existing seating. Pillows are also very versatile—they can be contrasting or complementary, plain or detailed—and they are relatively inexpensive. If large enough, pillows can even be scattered on the floor and used as casual seating.

S L I P C O V E R S

Slipcovered furniture is at the heart of the Shabby Chic style. Slipcovers can be made to look sleek or frilly, fancy or plain, depending upon the fabric and whether it has detailing, such as ruffles or welts (see Chapter 4, "Fabrics"). Myriad fabric and detail choices, ease of care, and their homey look make slipcovers my primary choice for new or old furniture.

Slipcovers are washable, so they offer the utmost in convenience and practicality. Like blue jeans or sweat-shirts, slipcovers become more cozy and individual with each washing, and allow furniture to be lived on rather than merely looked at, to be used freely rather than cautiously. Marked by the feeling of being handed down and touched by the factors of real life—dog

BELOW LEFT: When cutting fabric for a chair like the upholsterer is doing, the fitting is crucial. I prefer oversized slipcovers to allow for extra tucking, but sometimes, as in the case of more modern, streamlined furniture shapes, a tight fit is more appropriate.

BELOW RIGHT: When slipcovering a chair, the chair is measured first. Then, like an haute couture gown, the fabric is custom-cut to size. Once cut, the fabric is pin-fitted to the chair to make sure it fits, then removed and sewn into a slipcover, like this one at an upholsterer's.

PAGES 138–139: This is the type of squashy, floppy sofa I love. I call this one of matte lassé the Squadgey because it's so cushy and enveloping. When washed, the texture of the slipcover becomes even more inviting.

PAGES 140–141: The quintessential Shabby Chic sofa with smooshy feather-down seats.

hairs, a spilled glass of wine, an ink stain—accidents are taken in stride when they happen on a washable slipcovered sofa. If a stain doesn't come out, you can add a throw or pillow, or replace the damaged panel with a new piece of the same fabric. If I have trouble finding the same fabric, I often use a completely different fabric, but along with replacing the damaged panel, I balance out the look by adding the new fabric to other parts of the chair or sofa as well.

Today, slipcovers are not limited to just cotton or denim. When I first started my business, a washable slipcover made of a classic upholstery fabric such as velvet or chenille was almost unheard of. Now there are an array of fabrics that not only can be washed but that gain a whole new desirable texture and character as a result. After washing, damasks become more two-dimensional or puckered, chenilles gain a relaxed feel, and chintzes lose their stiff glean and become smooth. But not every material is conducive to laundering, however. Running embossed velvets or moirés through a washing machine can ruin their delicate patterns. And shrinkage is something to be aware of when measuring your fabric. Avoid laundering colors such as deep blues and bright reds as they tend to run.

If you have trouble finding a fabric in the exact color you want, you can always experiment with dyeing your own at home. An inexpensive way to obtain a color you can't find elsewhere is to buy a cotton sheet and some fabric dyes from the drugstore. Experiment with small amounts of material and dye before you actually work with the sheet. Once you achieve the color you're after, you can have the sheet fashioned into a slipcover.

Other ways to save money on slipcovering include mixing pricier fabrics with less expensive ones. The more visible back cushions, arms, and skirt of a chair or sofa can be covered in a silk-screened floral print for a hundred dollars a yard, while the seat cushions, back, and sides can be covered in a white denim for fifteen dollars a yard. The resulting look is a comfy, quiltlike look.

Another advantage to slipcovered furniture is that it does not lock you into one look all year round. You can have two different sets of slipcovers—a denim or cotton for summer, and velvet, chenille, or damask for winter. Having two sets is also convenient when your slipcovers are being laundered: You're never stuck with bare furniture—though you might want to consider whether the upholstery underneath the slipcovers is something you can live with while the covers are being washed. Just be sure that the existing upholstered fabric is of a lighter color than the slipcover to prevent it from showing through when the slipcover is on.

The fresh simplicity of stripes is perfect for slipcovers for outdoor furniture. I chose a red and white cotton, which has faded pleasantly over time, to cover my beach lounges. I never press the covers—the wrinkles and rumples add to the easy charm.

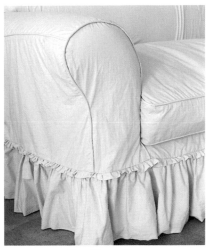

Double ruffle.

Box pleat.

Kick pleat.

Floppy ruffle.

SLIPCOVERING
BASICS

There are some basic guidelines to follow in order to insure that your slipcover fits well and that you get the look you envision. The following are tips to keep in mind whether you are making your own slipcover or having it done professionally.

1. Measure the piece of furniture to be covered. Generally, a six-foot-long by three-foot-deep sofa takes anywhere from twenty to twenty-five yards of fabric; an average love seat, about fifteen to seventeen yards; a chaise lounge, thirteen to seventeen yards; a chair six to twelve yards (these measurements include pillows); an ottoman, two to four yards. Keep in mind that yardage needed for slipcovers is always a little more than that needed for upholstery due to the slipcovers' looser fit. Fabric can range in cost from $10 to $110 a yard, and labor anywhere from $150 to $650 per piece, depending upon its size.

2. Choose your fabric and make sure it's prewashed to allow for shrinkage and to give it a softer texture, if that is your preference. Damasks and chenilles, for example, can shrink up to 25 percent. If you're using a fabric with a repeating pattern, it's very important to buy extra yardage for matching up the design. Extra fabric also needs to be factored in to allow for the lining of skirts and to have excess material for tucking in at the back and sides as well, to achieve the oversized slipcover look I prefer.

   For more formal or streamlined furniture, however, a tailored fit is more appropriate. If you want the piece to stay sleek, as is the case in more contemporary styles, you should have the slipcover dry cleaned rather than washed, as this creates the look of upholstered furniture but still offers the functionality of a slipcover.

3. Decide if you want piping around the cushions and what type of skirt and ruffle treatment you want, if any. There are a variety of different ruffle styles to chose from, including kick pleats, box pleats, double ruffles, and flanges. The amount of total fabric you'll need will be influenced by the type of ruffle you choose. If your chair or sofa has interesting legs, you might consider letting them show. If that's the case, as it often is with more modern shapes, then you may want a shorter skirt or no skirt at all.

4. Have the fabric fitted to the piece of furniture. Most slipcover suppliers make house calls. Some will take the furniture back with them to be covered, while others will take the fabric only and return with the finished slipcover for the final fitting.

5. Make sure the edges of your slipcovers are overlocked—that is, overlapped and resewn for reinforcement, especially if you're going to be washing your slipcovers rather than having them dry cleaned. Overlocking prevents fraying, although the process is expensive and can add as much as an additional one-third to labor costs.

S T U F F I N G S

Though not visible, the stuffings of chairs and couches are crucial to their comfort and longevity—a factor not to be overlooked whether you're buying ready- or custom-made furniture. While older sofas and couches have springs as their basis of support, most seat cushions today are made of a piece of synthetic foam core, which is available in a range of firmnesses, from super soft to extra firm. The foam is then enveloped by softer cotton, feathers and/or down, and some-times Dacron to make it more cushy. To make your sofa or chair last longer, it's important to change the foam every few years. You can buy foam core at many fabric stores or you can have an uphol-sterer change the foam for you. The back pillows of a couch or chair, as well as freestanding pillows, which don't need to offer as much support, don't require the foam core and can be made entirely of softer feathers and down—my favorite stuffing material.

Feathers and down, used by most high-quality cushion makers, are generally considered to be most desirable stuffings. Because feathers and down can conform to different body shapes, they create a more squashy feeling than synthetic polyester or

RIGHT TOP: The stuffings of this nineteenth-century Danish sofa—hay, flax, burlap, linen, jute, and horse hair, which are no longer used as stuffings—reveal its age. Today, various stuffings can be mixed to achieve different degrees of softness and hardness, as taste dictates.

RIGHT: Shown here are piles of different sofa and chair stuffings— synthetic, cotton, and kapok. Today, most cushions are a combination of different stuffings. Most commonly, a foam cushion is surrounded by cotton or down to create a firm center and soft outer layer.

OPPOSITE: The type of stuffing used in a chair or sofa is as important as the piece's structure and fabric covering. Fine feathers and down, considered to be the most desirable stuffing for cushions today, are used at most high-quality cushion makers like this one, where the feathers fly. For seat cushions, which require more support, the feathers usually surround some type of foam cushion, while back pillows are often made entirely of feathers and down.

urethane foam, both of which have less give. Made from the fine, soft feathers that keep the under-bellies of geese or ducks warm, down is more expensive than regular feathers. Varying the proportion of down to feathers in a cushion creates not only a difference in feel, but can also keep costs lower.

When making decisions about stuffing, try out a variety of cushions from super-soft to extra-firm to find out what your individual needs are. But whichever your preference, don't ignore stuffing, as it's critical to the longevity and comfort of your furniture.

Whether leather, wicker, or slipcovered, I look for comfort, quality, ease of use, and a certain aesthetic appeal or character in seating—the same qualities that are essential, in fact, to almost every aspect of my home decor philosophy.

6
LIGHTS
&
LIGHTING

Whether subtle or bright, ambient or accent, cool or warm, light dramatically influences the mood of a home. Lighting has the almost magical ability to enhance a beautifully decorated room or to make a room that may be lacking in some way appear more flattering.

Lighting serves an important array of purposes from room to room and from moment to moment. A front entryway for example, should offer warm, inviting, welcoming light; a kitchen, light that is functional for cooking; a bedroom, various options of light for either relaxing, reading, or getting dressed by. The quality of light one desires changes both according to need and personal preference.

If you find a chandelier you want to buy but it has a few missing pieces, it may be worthwhile to purchase some new crystal or glass and do the work yourself. Depending on their size and quality, and whether they're glass or crystal, vintage or new, these replacement pieces range in price anywhere from a few to twenty dollars. An old cabinet serves as a storage space for chandelier parts (BELOW LEFT). A chandelier in need of some repair (OPPOSITE). Work in progress— a pile of crystal and some bulb holders wait to be added to the fixture (BELOW RIGHT). The finished product (PAGE 155).

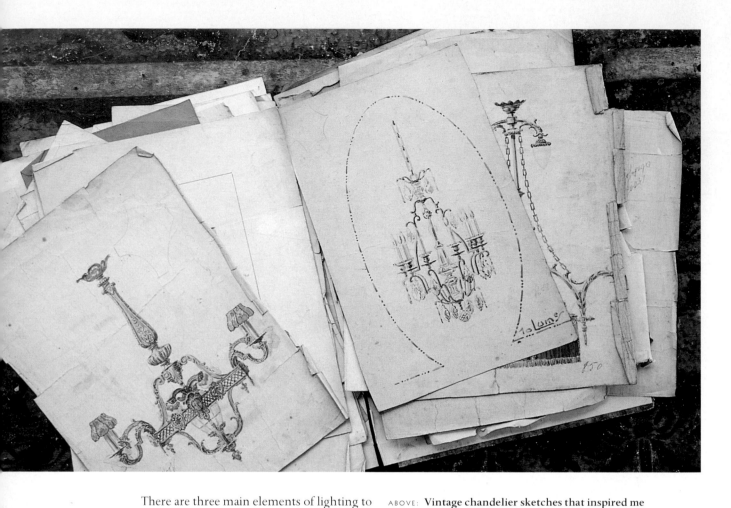

There are three main elements of lighting to consider—fixture, function, and quality—and my approach to them is simple. The fixture should be attractive, unless it's a hidden source of light. The quality (determined by intensity, type, and placement of the light fixture) should be both pleasing to the eye and fulfill the intended function, that is, it should be suitable for reading or establish a mood, and so on. Natural light is important, too—be it sunshine pouring through windows or the comforting mood of fire and candlelight, both of which are among my favorite ways to light any room.

ABOVE: **Vintage chandelier sketches that inspired me to restore some old fixtures.**

FIXTURES

ighting fixtures can be attractive accessories that serve as decorative aspects of a room, regardless of the quality of light they emanate. Sometimes the physical structure of the light itself is determined by the function for which it is intended. The form of a chandelier, for example, does not make it conducive to reading by, while a desk lamp is not structured to create a warm, ambient light for a living room.

Crystal chandeliers, intricate wrought-iron Italian sconces, colored glass lamp shades that give off a warm glow, interesting vintage lamps made of porcelain or glass, or casual wicker lamps—these are the types of lighting fixtures that work best in humble Shabby Chic environments. Chandeliers and sconces, electrical or candlelit, add glamour and formality to otherwise casual surroundings. They can serve as excellent focal points of a room and make dramatic statements when hung low or in unexpected places. Colored glass shades or pieces of colored glass set into hanging fixtures

OPPOSITE: Wicker lamps have a fresh look and can make a room feel a little more casual instantly. Here, a collection of wicker lamps from my own home in various weaves—loose, tight, and basket.

ABOVE: A flea market angel adorns the base of this vintage lamp with custom shades in the home of Chantall Cloutier. The amber hue of the shades gives the soft light an even warmer feel.

are attractive because they seem to glow from within and also create interesting patterns of colored light on other surfaces. I like wicker lamps because they have a fresh and natural quality, fit in well with casual settings, and can provide contrast in formal settings to create a more welcoming atmosphere.

Flea markets and yard sales are great resources for discovering vintage lighting fixtures with lots of character. Don't walk away from a wicker lamp just because the weaving is torn. Don't ignore a broken chandelier or lamp that you love only because the wiring doesn't work. Wicker can be restored (see

Chapter 3, "Hidden Treasures and Inspirations"), and wiring problems can be fixed easily by an electrician. Cracks in a metal chandelier can be fixed by a welder.

With regard to electrical fixtures, I suggest having an electrician look at any used lighting fixture as a precaution against sparks, shorts, or fires, even if the piece seems to work perfectly. Of course, the restoration costs of rewiring vary drastically and are dependent upon the intricacy of the job. Internal wiring costs more, for example, than external wiring. You can expect to pay anywhere from forty to two hundred dollars to have a chandelier rewired. A less expensive alternative is to transform a lighting fixture into a candleholder by removing all the wiring and placing candles in the bulb sockets. If there are cracks in the sockets, adding small holders made of glass or metal will help prevent the candle wax from dripping, or you can use dripless candles.

To avoid fire hazards, be sure the chandelier is placed well away from fabrics, wood, and other inflammable materials and avoid leaving candles unattended.

When replacing lamp parts, keep quality and authenticity in mind. Cloth-covered cords and brass pull chains are more appealing than plastic ones. If you're replacing light bulbs, frosted ones not only look better but offer a gentler radiance. If a chandelier is missing a few pieces of crystal or has colored pieces and you'd prefer an all-clear look, this too can be corrected with new crystal or glass pieces. If the job is simply a matter of replacing a few pieces, you might attempt it yourself. But if the job entails an entire re-creation, you may want to reconsider the purchase. Such restoration is not only costly but finding a qualified specialist in what is now becoming a lost art can be difficult and time-consuming.

Sunlight coming through this jeweled Moroccan candle lamp makes it a terrific lighting fixture, even in the daytime. Another of the lamp's features is that it works equally as well outdoors as in. Here, it hangs over my sun deck, its cool blue and green jewels mimicking the tones of the sea.

FUNCTION
AND QUALITY

The function of a particular light—whether it be for reading, cooking, or creating a relaxing environment—in turn determines the quality of light that should emanate from it. The quality of light is comprised of the type of light, its brightness or intensity, its warmth or coolness, and its placement. The two most common types of home lighting are fluorescent—the flat, cool light commonly found in kitchens—and incandescent—either halogen, a harsh, bright light often used as desk lamps, or tungsten, a warmer, lamp light commonly found in living rooms and bedrooms. The brightness or intensity of a light is determined by the wattage of the bulb and can be altered by putting the light on a dimmer switch. Available at hardware stores for about twenty dollars, dimmer switches are easy to install.

OPPOSITE: A "chandelier" lamp from the forties lends elegance to a simple white bedside table in the home of Philomena Giusti, imbuing the room with a soft, warm light.

LEFT: Not only is the type of light that a source gives off crucial to creating a mood, but the look of the lamp or light itself is important, too. The faded grandeur of this flea market crystal chandelier in Jennifer Nicholson's front foyer sets up the ambiance for her entire house. As a personal touch, Nicholson added a tiny glass ballerina ornament.

ABOVE: This intricate iron chandelier found at a flea market hangs amid the vines on Jennifer Nicholson's front porch and is the type of warm touch that makes a good first impression and sets the tone for the decorative style within the house.

I love cool, flat, clean light with an almost bluish tone. Whether a light is cool or warm depends on the type of bulb and its intensity but also on its surroundings. If a room is done in hues such as greens, silvers, grays, and blues, like the floral guest room of Tony and Donna Scott, you're more apt to achieve a cool blue versus a warm rosy quality of light. Light reflected off stone surfaces and windows facing lots of greenery or covered in cool, sheer shades are also ways to attain this calming, tranquil quality of light.

The placement of a lighting source—whether direct or indirect—can also make a vast difference in the perceived depth of a room and its overall ambiance. Lighting, like most other aspects of home decorating, is about balance, a compromise between aesthetics and function. Just as I don't believe in decor that is precious or ostentatious, I steer away from lighting that is overly dramatic or decorative. Even when coming from artificial sources, lighting should appear as natural as possible, blending in with, rather than standing out from, the comfortable, practical, livable aspects of a home.

TOP LEFT: Walls along staircases are opportune places for whimsical or welcoming accessories to greet passersby. This delicately carved metal wall sconce depicting a female nude with a horn in the 1926 home of Tony and Donna Scott dates from the residence of its former owner, John Barrymore.

LEFT: The empty area between two doorways is an unexpected spot for a touch of whimsy. A floral toile wall sconce from the forties, set between bunches of dried flowers, lends color to this space in Philomena Giusti's home.

OPPOSITE: Sometimes one great piece can inspire the look of an entire room. A relic from the home's former owner, John Barrymore, this grand, intricately detailed, angel and floral Dresden chandelier from the palace of Archduke Francis Ferdinand sets the mood for Tony and Donna Scott's formal living room.

OPPOSITE: A palm tree hanging lamp dating from the forties lends an air of whimsy to Tony and Donna Scott's guest house bedroom.

ABOVE: Ceilings, very important to creating a sense of height and space in a room, can add real design interest, too. Tin ceilings, though expensive, give a room a rich feeling and make great backdrops for beautiful lights. I love the play of pattern upon pattern created by this crystal chandelier against the embossed tin ceiling shown here.

FOLLOWING PAGES: Jennifer Nicholson decorated an entire corner of her home around this unusual vintage Czechoslovakian chandelier with glass in the shape and color of grapes. The first piece she bought for her home, it illustrates how lighting sources can be aesthetic as well as functional.

FESTIVA
MAXIMA

JULES

7
—
FLOWERS

Real flowers and their abstract representations are one of the most important characteristics of the Shabby Chic style and an essential ingredient for creating the simple, unaffected look I love. As reminders of the natural evolution of life and the beauty of all its stages—from glorious budding and blossoming to delicate withering and fading—flowers bring the outdoors into the home, adding life, color, and fragrance.

PRECEDING PAGES: Because of their undefined, almost blurry shape, muted coloring, and soft texture, peonies, available in many varieties, are good flowers for casual arrangements.

LEFT: Unexpected colors, a bit of humor, or an offbeat pattern on a vase can prevent a floral arrangement from being too romantic. The lively, circuslike polka dots of this glass bowl offset the dreaminess of the roses and lend the arrangement a bit of whimsy and modernism.

OPPOSITE: Large, loose arrangements can lend real impact without being overpowering, as demonstrated by these giant white poppies paired with eucalyptus leaves. This arrangement dominates the corner of the room while also blending in with its surroundings, picking up on the green floral print of the chairs and sofa and complementing the white floral oil painting behind it.

FRESH FLOWERS

armer's markets, fields, gardens, meadows, nurseries, and flower marts in major cities are prime locations for finding quality fresh flowers. Farmer's markets are my choice, as they are so accessible and usually offer a mishmash of meadow and field flowers that look less cultivated than flowers from other outlets. Large bunches can be purchased for anywhere from two to ten dollars. City flower marts are usually restricted to those with wholesale accounts, so unless you have a connection, they can be frustrating to use. I try to avoid hothouse flowers because they tend to look too artificial. Small imperfections and slight irregularities give flowers a more individual, natural feel.

Varieties of flowers that serve as good basics for the kind of bountiful arrangements I love include bearded iris, garden roses of all varieties, lavender, lilacs, Casablanca lilies, camellias, tulips, peonies, delphinium, hollyhocks, and dahlias. Flowers good for floating in bowls of water include lilies, orchids, roses, and gardenias.

Rounding out bouquets with fillers gives them more depth and fullness. Some of my favorite fillers include eucalyptus leaves (silver dollar or knife blade work better than spiral varieties), lemon

leaves, Queen Anne's lace, and flowering fruit branches, such as peach, apple, and cherry—but almost anything tall with interesting branches or leaves works well. Some fillers are available at farmer's markets. Others can often be found in your own backyard or on a nature walk.

I prefer large and abundant arrangements in wide-lipped vases filled to bursting. Though bright flowers can be dramatic, I usually select more subdued hues, like dusty pinks, blues, laven-

LEFT: Orchids work well in sophisticated settings and bespeak an elegant beauty. Most orchids should be kept in light, airy soil or bark and misted as much as possible.

OPPOSITE: Just as the natural irregularities of flowers add to their beauty, imperfections in vases can hold appeal. The chipped flowers on this porcelain vase imbue it with a wilted feel that echoes the appearance of the roses inside. If such imperfections are too distracting, they can be covered up economically with a bit of nail polish.

For me, arranging flowers is not work but one of my most enjoyable pastimes. I love playing with roses in particular. If possible, work where you'll have lots of room to spread out.

1. JARDINS DES BAGATELLE
2. ANGEL FACE
3. CALICO
4. HEINRICH MUNCH
5. ABRACADABRA
6. SOUTH SEAS
7. WINCHESTER CATHEDRAL
8. PRISTINE
9. GRAHAM THOMAS
10. CHARMIAN
11. ARLENE FRANCIS
12. BROADWAY
13. MISS ALL AMERCIAN BEAUTY
14. PARTY TIME
15. COTTAGE ROSE
16. PERDITA
17. PARADISE

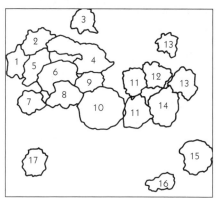

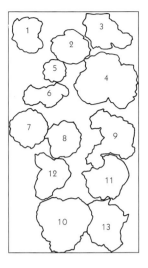

1. PEACH BLOSSOM
2. LEANDER
3. PEAUDOULE
4. LUCETA
5. SILVER SHADOWS
6. LILAC ROSE
7. COTTAGE ROSE
8. PERDITA
9. LEANDER
10. ENGLISH GARDEN
11. GEORGIA
12. PRISTINE
13. WIMI

A giant bunch of garden roses is eye-catching wherever it is placed. Garden roses have bigger blooms and are more fragrant than the typical hothouse variety sold in most shops. Rather than being bred to look identical, garden-rose blooms are individual, with several buds or branches attached to each stem in a unique pattern. When placed in a group, the particular characteristics of the roses become all the more exaggerated.

ders, and creams and arrange them in monochromatic or subtle color variations. In keeping with the imperfect, comfortable look of the furniture and fabrics that appeal to me, I'm attracted to flower arrangements that are asymmetrical, irregular, wildly shaped, and loosely, almost haphazardly, assorted. An arrangement should never be so studied that it dominates the flowers themselves. I much prefer random arrangements of flowers that can be enjoyed from all angles, like the flowers growing naturally in a garden. To keep an arrangement from becoming one-sided, I rotate the container as I work. I gravitate toward vases with unique details, preferably old ones with cracks and chips caused by the vagaries of time. Occasionally, an old vase will not be watertight, but that is a problem easily solved. Professional liners can be purchased inexpensively at most floral supply outlets. I often just place a glass jar filled with water inside the vase.

Flowers need not be confined to short periods of display. The evolution of their life cycle, even in their later stages of subtle wilting and slight drooping, is a part of their appeal. Discarding an arrange-ment after a few days does not allow for an appreciation of its graceful aging, which can be as dramatic and beautiful as its peak, fresh from the garden display. I like to let petals that have fallen from an arrangement to the table below remain there as part of the look. Gathering the fallen petals in a porce-lain or glass bowl (with or without water), using them in satchels of potpourri, or drying them are other ways of appreciating the loveliness of flowers longer. I also love the feeling of bringing the outside in with a potted rosebush. Not only is it a creative alternative to more predictable floral displays, it ulti-mately lasts longer and is less expensive. Costing anywhere from eighteen to twenty dollars each, rose-bushes typically last for about two weeks before needing to be replanted outside.

While flower arrangements are common in living rooms and dining rooms, placing them in unconventional, less-expected locations can add new life to any space. An arrangement of flowers might pop up in a forgotten corner, a hallway, under the staircase, or at the edge of the bathtub. Fresh flowers—or those made of silk, velvet, or linen—can also be a wonderful surprise on a plain wrapped present, as an adornment for a frame, or decoration on a birthday cake. For gifts, I often just use a plain brown paper bag, adding flowers or vintage milliner's trinkets in the shape of fruits and berries, and scraps of fabric, lace, string or raffia as trim. Old hat or vintage shoe boxes, which can be found at flea markets and secondhand shops, can also make very pretty containers for presents.

Fabric flowers can be used in place of real ones if they are made of high-quality material. Linen, velvet, and silk, for example, have the ability to mimic the soft folds and frays of real flowers.

ABOVE: Flowers, whether real or faux, make attractive accents for presents. Some butcher paper or paper bags, scraps of old fabric, ribbon or lace from around the house, and a bit of raffia or string are all you need to wrap a lovely gift.

OPPOSITE: Fresh flowers from the garden are an inexpensive, easy way to decorate cakes. The large roses atop this green marzipan cake make all the difference between ordinary and unique ornamentation.

FLOWER CUTTING
AND CARE

- ☐ Have water immediately available when you are cutting flowers and put them in the water as soon as possible. For maximum freshness, flowers should never be out of water for very long.

- ☐ Cut stems with a sharp knife at a diagonal, scraping the sides an inch or so above the cut to maximize the amount of surface that can absorb water. If the stem is thick or woody, make a few crisscross cuts and scrape off an inch or two of bark up the stem so water can penetrate more easily.

- ☐ Remove all leaves below the vase line and any excess foliage. The idea is to steer the water to the flower, not to leaves that you can't see. Remove blossoms and leaves as they die to conserve energy for the remaining flowers, unless, of course, you like the look of the wilting flowers.

- ☐ Always use clean water and add new water often, keeping the stems submerged, even if you change the water completely or move the flowers to a different container. Some stems are very delicate and can close up their cuts after only a few moments of air exposure.

- ☐ To revive flowers that have become droopy, completely submerge them in cold water for about an hour. This works for any flower that does not have a fuzzy texture (fuzzy-textured flowers tend to get water spots). Misting leaves in hot weather can also help refresh them.

- ☐ Bleach can act as a preservative for flowers by keeping the water clean and preventing bacteria growth and malodorous fumes. But don't overdo it. A teaspoonful is sufficient. Professional floral additives, which inhibit bacteria, stimulate growth, and condition water can be purchased at florists or floral supply stores. Bleach is also good for cleaning containers thoroughly.

White tulips are a simple classic that works everywhere.
Here Chantall Cloutier uses them to lighen up the richness of this dark corner of cobalt bowls and candles.

FLORAL
REPRESENTATIONS

Oil and watercolor paintings of flowers are one of my favorite accessories for a room. Good examples tend to come from the mid- to late-Victorian era and depict flowers scattered randomly across the canvas rather than in the formal, stylized vase arrangements paired with birds or fruit that were predominant in the twenties. "Yard longs"—named for their size—are relatively rare, horizontal floral paintings or prints, mainly from the nineteenth century. The proportion of a yard long makes a good choice for hanging over couches or beds, in long hallways, or behind tables. Floral paint-

ings have become extremely popular in the last few years, and so are much harder to find and more expensive than they used to be, although good ones can be found occasionally at flea markets.

I try to avoid paintings that require restoration, although small flaws can be covered up with minimal work. If a canvas has a small rip, as opposed to a missing piece, you can smudge a bit of oil paint that matches the color in the painting onto the front side of a piece of acid-free tape, then fasten the tape to the back of the canvas. Larger flaws can be repaired professionally, beginning at a cost of about two hundred dollars. One positive aspect of paintings with flaws is that you can bargain for better deals.

Most of the floral paintings I'm attracted to are from the turn of the century, when artists created less formal compositions. Although I don't look for works by registered artists, sometimes I'll happen upon a work that is by a well-known painter such as these pink roses (OPPOSITE BOTTOM) by Marie Johansen. Sometimes, a painting doesn't require a frame at all, such as this slightly more formal composition of fruits and flowers (OPPOSITE TOP).

BELOW A frame can be as much a part of an artwork as the canvas. The size of this frame, made from an old architectural molding, almost overshadows this tiny painting of a rose in my living room. Chipped and peeling, the frame adds a feeling of glamour and delicate decay.

OPPOSITE: These teacups with "chintz" patterns and floral designs inside as well as outside are Jennifer Nicholson's favorites. Here she uses them informally, with mismatched dishes and colors that complement one another. The worn pink table's scratches and cracks are left to create an interesting contrast with the dainty floral teacups, fine linen napkins, and silver. Nicholson collects cups from small shops, flea markets, and antique sales all over the country. She much prefers these to perfectly matching pieces, which she finds to be too stiff and uniform. (See Resource Guide.)

ABOVE: The unique qualities of this silver teapot that my friend inherited from her grandmother are its delicate floral etchings and hinged lid. The creamer is covered with a shell and bead-trimmed net from Africa. The cracks in the wooden tray and the tiny reproduction roses added to its edge give this tea setting a wonderful, crumbling, shabby mood.

LEFT: Beautiful form and useful function merge perfectly in this delicate, hand-made rose teacup belonging to Jennifer Nicholson. The muted color, wilted look of the petals, and the rosebud handles are examples of the types of details that make a piece exceptional.

Old architectural wooden moldings, their paint cracked and peeling, make eye-catching frames with lots of character, though a canvas with no frame at all is also appealing in its simplicity. Glass can be used to protect watercolors, but do not place it on oil paintings, as they need to breathe.

I often look for floral details on vintage wooden furniture, whether painted, etched, or in relief. Though some artists are masters at adding floral details to furniture, I much prefer pieces with original flower work—as evidenced by cracked, faded, and peeling paint.

Fabrics with floral patterns and accessories such as chandeliers, napkin rings, candlesticks, wastebaskets, lamps, and dishes adorned with flower shapes or painted floral details are additional ways to bring the appeal of flowers to a room. When combining different floral looks, a few well-chosen objects work better than an overabundance of knickknacks, and soft tones and subdued mixes work better than loud colors and sharp contrasts. In my living room and bedroom, for example, the use of complementary tones and subtleties of print and detail help prevent the floral motif from taking over, enabling the look to enhance rather than dominate the room.

Whether real or represented, flowers are a crucial element of interior decor, not only because of their natural beauty but because they enliven the static of the indoors with the more mutable, ephemeral, and sensory quality of the outdoors.

RIGHT: The decayed, delicate look
of these dried roses is as beautiful as
that of fresh flowers. To keep dried
flowers from crumbling, spray them
with hair spray and handle them
gently. Like real flowers, they can be
used in arrangements or to adorn
hats or gifts, or can be hung simply
in bunches from the wall.

FOLLOWING PAGE: Frilly, edged
cotton tablecloths in pale colors left
out to dry and benefit from fading
by the sun make a lovely sight in
their own right, surrounded by rose
petals.

RESOURCE GUIDE

AA-Abbington Affiliates Inc.
Dept V.H. 26
2149 Utica Ave.
Brooklyn, NY 11234
718-258-8333
Page 41: Tin ceilings

Aga John Carpet
8687 Melrose Ave.
Suite B 130
Los Angeles, CA 90069
310-659-4444
Pages 18–19: Rug

Blackman Cruise
800 N. La Cienega Blvd.
Los Angeles, CA 90069
310-657-9228
Page 16: Apothecary jars,
    Indian stone bowls

Bountiful
1335 Abbot Kinney
Venice, CA 90291
310-450-3620
Pages 42–43: French leather club
    chairs
Page 44: Jars
Page 83: Wicker repair

Larson Carpet
1480 Ridgeway St.
Union, NJ 07083
908-686-7203
Page 17: Rug

Liz's Antique Hardware
453 South La Brea Blvd.
Los Angeles, CA 90036
310-939-4403
Pages 92–93: Assorted vintage
    hardware, porcelain, casters,
    wheels, wooden drawer pulls

Maison
148 S. La Brea Blvd.
Los Angeles, CA 90036
213-935-3157
Page 64: Moroccan glassware,
    French glassware

Marmalade
710 Montana Ave.
Santa Monica Ave.
Santa Monica, CA 90403
310-395-9196
Page 66: Catering
Page 190: Catering

Odalisque
7278 Beverly Blvd.
Los Angeles, CA 90036
213-933-9100
Page 45: Nineteenth-century
    100 percent cotton bedding
Page 129: Nineteenth-century
    100 percent cotton drapery

Room with a View
1600 Montana Ave.
Santa Monica, CA 90403
310-998-5858
Page 6: Amber glassware
Page 16: Towel and soap
Page 59: Cutlery
Page 62: Dinnerware

Shabby Chic, Inc.
1013 Montana Ave.
Santa Monica, CA 90403
310-394-1975
Page 2: "Triangle Chair"
Pages 8–9: Cream chintz daybed
Page 13: "Curly Chair"
Pages 14–15: "B&B Chair," "Elegant
    Sofa"—fabric: Pale Bunch
    Summer on Oyster—**Shabby
    Chic Fabrics**
Page 17: "Swayback Sofa," "Mod
    Chair"
Pages 18–19: Blue floral slipcovers
Page 47: Linen/bedding from **Shabby
    Chic Home Collection, T-Shirt
    Collection**
Page 122: Petite Bloom Fall on Butter
    Linen—**Shabby Chic Fabrics**
    Watermark Spring on Butter
    Linen—**Shabby Chic Fabrics**
    Pale Bunch Summer on Oyster—
    Shabby Chic Fabrics
Page 130: Shabby Chic Home
    Collector
Page 136: "Large Chaise" in white
    denim, shades

*The author would also like to acknowledge
contributions from:*

Nina Krivanek: Flower stylist

Pauline Gravier and Liz Sharp:
Decor style assistants

RACHEL ASHWELL'S
SHABBY CHIC

TREASURE HUNTING
& DECORATING GUIDE

150%
enlarge...

for dresser,
in bedroom.

Argile Rose   Lavande Grisée   Vert

Rose Burgundy 1   Lavender   Vert

Rose Burgundy 2   Sky Blue   Pine

Wine   Sea Blue   Peach

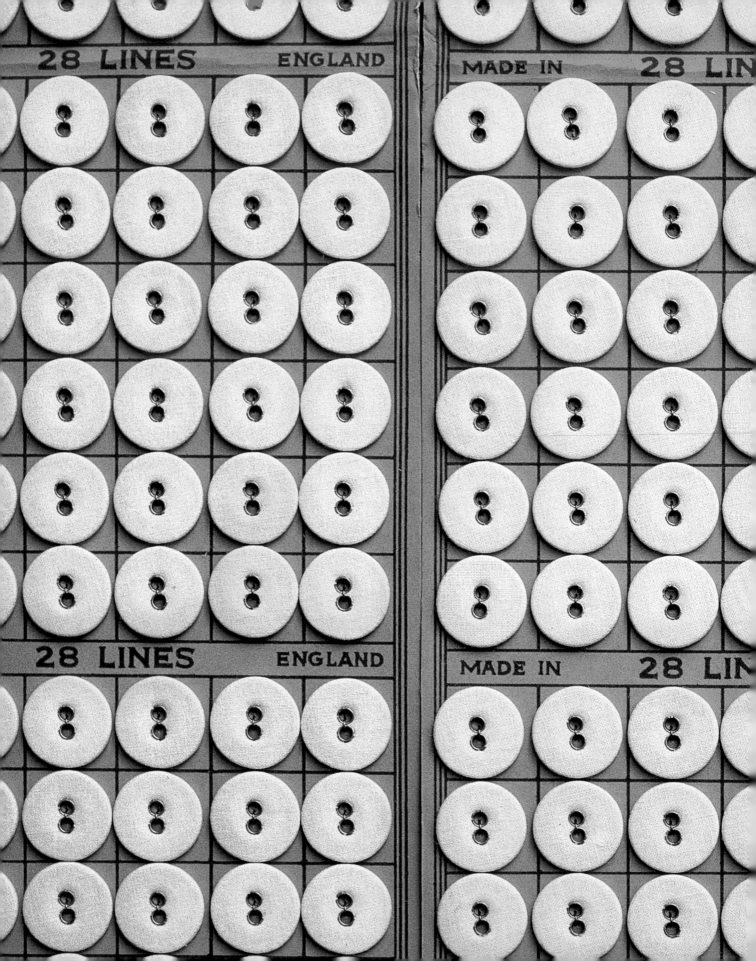

CONTENTS

ACKNOWLEDGMENTS

Shabby Chic is about comfort and awareness of what is truly important and valuable. This description is also true of the following people to whom I owe thanks and appreciation for their various contributions to this book.

Thank you, Cathy, for your lovely photographs and for bringing me Wynn.

Wynn, for your patience, support, and your photographs, too.

Gabrielle and Cliff, for understanding my vision.

Deborah, my sister, for your wonderful, charming illustrations.

Annabel Davis-Goff, for giving grace to my mumbled text.

Brendan and Rochelle, for your truly endless perseverance with the captions.

Mari, Rodney, Tom , Elliot, Julie, Sonny, Marilyn, Georgann, Nina, Jeanne, Jenni, Helena, Linda, Mark, Damon, Kevin, Kinga, Jeff, Miguel, Julian, Manuel, Helen, Petty, Terry, Camilla, Rosetta, Kristin, Kerry, Stephanie, Claudine, and Lupe.
Your support of Shabby Chic allows me to do what I love to do.

Linda, for understanding my love of the shade of pink.

Tinda, for your attention to detail.

Angelica, Jenny, and Judith, thank you for loving what I love.

Andrea and Bruce, M.L., Sue, Barry and Lili, Nina and Lou, Liz, and Karin, for welcoming me in to your homes and sharing your worlds.

Ted, for your unique point of view that inspires me.

And lastly, thank you to Lili and Jake, for understanding the days of my preoccupation with the "book."

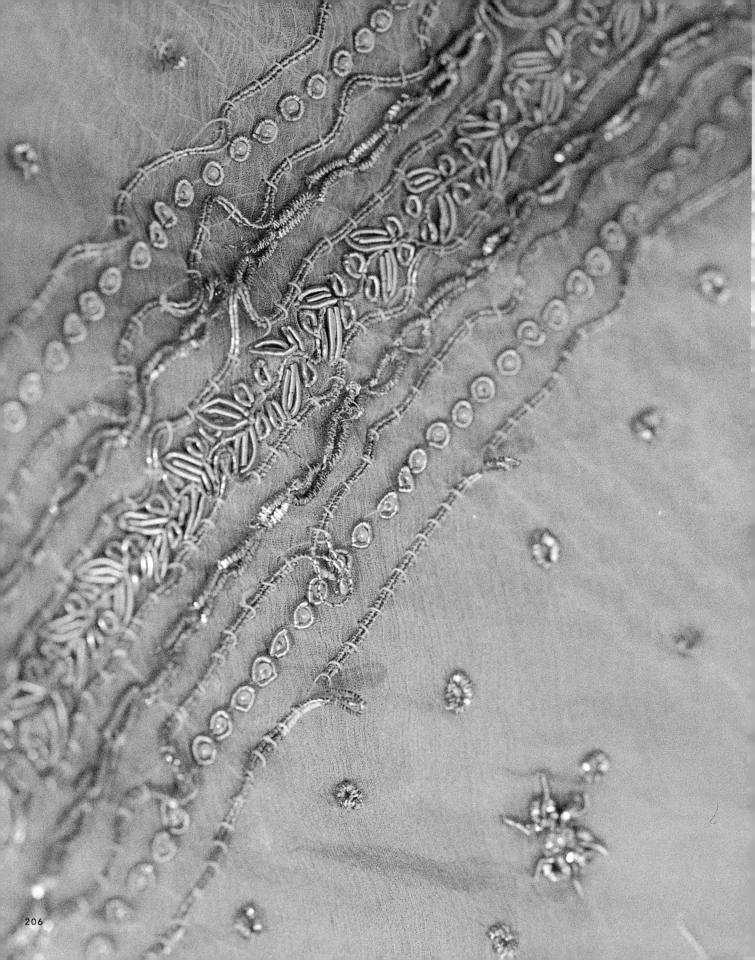

INTRODUCTION
introduction

Early mornings at flea markets: a childhood memory. I still feel that flutter of excitement—not entirely acquisitive—that I used to feel as a small girl, arriving at the flea market with my parents on cold mornings. We would rise in the dark, dress sleepily, and hurried by my mother, we would arrive at the market as the vendors were unpacking their wares. I remember those vendors as though they were distant relatives. And I remember the smell of the cakes from the cafeteria, and the accelerated speed at which my father walked when he had the whiff of a treasure.

Now I live, with my own children, in Malibu, in a house where, when I wake, the sound of the ocean replaces the hum of traffic on the London street where I was born. And visits to a flea market are not only a voyage into the past of the object I inspect and sometimes buy and restore but a journey into my own childhood.

My mother bought, restored, and sold antique dolls and teddy bears. My father dealt in secondhand rare books. My parents took my sister and me with them on those flea-market Sunday mornings, and without planning it, they opened the door to a glimpse of cultural history. In doing so, they also gave me a head start in developing my "eye" and, later, the means of earning my living.

My mother would advertise in local newspapers around the country: "Dolls and teddy bears wanted." Before she set off to a prospective seller she would talk to him for a long time on the telephone, mostly to discuss the type of doll or bear offered for sale but also to be sure the owner was really ready to part with a childhood friend. My mother was not an aggressive buyer. She was honest about her intentions and would lovingly restore the dolls and bears, knowing that ultimately they would be sold—to (she hoped) good homes.

I can remember waiting in excited anticipation for her to come home from her buying trips. She usually traveled by train, with her finds packed in a suitcase or bags. After she had revived herself with a cup of tea, she would carefully unwrap the layers of tissue paper protecting the porcelain heads of the dolls. On a certain level, this was quite an intimate business. Often, as she unwrapped her purchases, sometimes she would tell me their history. After the dolls, she would unwrap their accessories. I was fascinated by the tiny clothes and scrunched-up silk flowers, hanging by threads from the straw hats and the matted wigs.

Dolls bloomers 19th

At this point, my mother would assess what could be saved, restored, or left as is. By watching this process of assessment, I developed the ability to judge items that cross my path.

I rarely wanted to own any of the treasures my mother brought home. But I was intrigued and developed an appreciation of quality, detail, patience, function, and beauty.

The imperfect dolls, often the less-fussy boy dolls, were my personal favorites. A doll with a cracked face or some fingers missing was the seed of the "imperfect beauty" that is an integral part of my taste today.

Victorian dolls hat and knitted booties

Once my mother had finished her assessment and checked for identification marks (on the dolls, usually an imprint on the back of the neck; on the bears, a tag on the ear), she would begin the restoration. She worked with a small network of women across London who each specialized in some aspect of a doll's wardrobe. One woman, a homeworker, made beautiful straw hats and lacy bonnets, always using authentic trim and buttons. Another made charming miniature leather shoes.

My mother sold the restored dolls and teddy bears from a booth in Camden Passage in north London. She would arrive, unwrap her prized possessions and display them proudly on the shelves that lined her booth. Her turnover was fast, for her work was appreciated, and she opened only two days a week. Her experience and taste told her just how much to restore something without overdoing it. She knew when a tear or a hole added to the charm of a doll or a bear. Most of her customers were women, and they would come from all over the world to buy from her. Often their children were grown, or they had given their own dolls away as children and were now seeking to replace them. Or they would come just to talk about their childhoods and to recount proudly how they had, in childhood, saved their dolls from destructive brothers. Men would sometimes stop by, too, for the teddy bears.

Money would eventually change hands, but almost as an afterthought. The ritual was infinitely more important than the money or the possession. There was an appreciation of history, an exchange of experiences, and the willingness to listen to someone else's story—moments that can never exist when buying from today's shopping malls and mail-order catalogues.

And then there was my father and his second-hand rare-book business. Originally led into the world of books by his appreciation for the written word, he also respected the fine leather bindings and admired the plates of the great illustrators Arthur Rackham, Kate Greenway, and Beatrix Potter. But what excited him most was the search. With speed and determination he would seek and ultimately find what he was searching for. I have vivid memories of trying to keep up with him, of how quickly his legs would carry him through crowds and the aisles of product.

As with my mother, the conversation that came with the exchange was of great interest and pleasure to him. I was in awe of his ability to see so quickly, to recognize treasures in the blink of an eye. I thank my father for passing that on to me.

FLEA MARKETS AND RESTORATION

What to look for and how to decorate with secondhand treasures

Celadon greens, mint and seafoam; dusty roses; ivories, creams, and faded grays; a touch of pale sky blue; crisp, clean whites. Worn damask, faded velvets, tea-stained florals, washed-out cotton prints, tattered lace, monogrammed linen. Worn grandeur, the incomplete, the neglected, the crumbling, the cracked, the mismatched, the wrinkled. Ruffles, gathers, tucking; scuffed, chipped, imperfect; scratched moldings, discarded beauty, peeling paint. This is Shabby Chic—the colors that make up my palette; the qualities that suggest things inherited rather than bought.

After color and character, I look for workmanship. Usually this means work done by hand: in furniture, tongue-in-groove joints; in dresses, hand stitching. My own taste centers on faded elegance, muted colors, worn moldings, honestly-come-by crackled paints.

I follow one more basic rule: Function. Everything I buy is functional (although often its function is one other than for which it was originally intended), and is bought with a thought of how it will blend with what I already own. I don't collect anything— no tchotchkes! It is important that you develop and define your taste. You may be fortunate enough to be born with a good "eye," but taste requires work, time, and experience. You will develop it by looking and paying attention, and by making a few mistakes.

It is early morning—a little after five o'clock—and I am arriving at a flea market. The vendors are still unpacking their wares. A glimpse of dusty celadon green catches my eye and I pause.

The green is the pottery base of a table lamp. The shade is exquisite. The cream silk has yellowed, and a ruffle of mottled fabric—the original cream alternating with infinitely faded pink—has worn though in places, although some tiny bows remain, peeking through the tattered tucks. The lining is split in many places but I don't care: I buy it. Shades with this detailing are among my favorite flea-market finds, but I am not put off by an unattractive or hopelessly damaged shade on a good base. A plain parchment or white linen shade, although in a completely different way, can bring the lamp back to life. (Although, however new or functional the wiring seems, I always have lamps professionally rewired.) In addition to table lamps, the stall contains sconces and chandeliers. Immediately my eye is drawn to a metal wall sconce, painted cream with green leaves and buds which add touches of pink. My palette! I am not discouraged by the worn metal or the chipped paint. The sconce would not be difficult to restore, but I like its shabby elegance and will probably leave it as it is. In addition to the rewiring I will need to replace the candle sleeves—not a difficult job. I buy it and ask the price of an alabaster table lamp but decide, after adding in the cost of rewiring, that it is too expensive. Nevertheless, I make a note of the lamp and its location. There are many interested customers at the stall, so I am in a weak bargaining position. If, when I return for the sconce at the end of my day, the lamp hasn't sold, the dealer may prefer to reduce the price rather than pack it up and take it home.

(previous spread)
My office. A site of both creativity and stress—no business functions without endless decision-making. It is important that my office be both practical and aesthetically pleasing. Clearly visible are reminders of Shabby Chic, aesthetically and functionally. A view of my past collections inspires my future projects. Glass covers a rough picnic table and allows photographs, sketches, and swatches to be displayed. Glass-fronted cabinets allow for easy viewing of fabrics. Repainted flea-market wicker chairs have some of my fabric designs tossed to them to test response. My full palette is spread throughout the room.

Before I leave I start my list, jotting down the purchases, how much they cost, and the location of the vendor who sold them. By the time I am finished, especially if I have had a successful day, I may have become a little vague about where I bought things. I move on.

Metal furniture is next; I am taken with the detailing on the weathered leg of a wrought-iron garden table. Its glass top is missing, but I am not deterred. The veined leaves are intricate and I can see that the piece is old. Peeling white paint reveals the scuffed iron beneath. I pick my way deeper into the booth where I see dilapidated bed frames, and I am drawn by the patina where the ivory paint has worn through to show traces of an earlier green. Swiftly I buy the bedstead, the garden table, and two similar but not matching iron garden chairs. The chairs will be delightful when I have painted them ivory and given them mushy down cushions covered in faded floral chintz—perhaps of autumnal pale blue, gray, and washed-out green leaves.

Over the years my eye has developed the ability to "edit" out irrelevant merchandise at flea markets. I no longer register the old lawn mowers or the fifties plastic furniture, so the next time I pause it is at a stall that always has a large selection of fabric.

I rarely leave this vendor empty-handed. It is here—among the worn velvets, the ruffled tablecloths, the tattered lace, the white-on-white bedspreads—that I will find the chintz for my newly purchased garden chairs. The chintz is just the way I like it: washed so many times that no trace of the glaze remains. I also buy a length of hand-blocked cotton print—rose on white with a green so faded it is almost gray. Not only are many of the fabrics this dealer offers not available new, but this is by far the most economical way of buying linen, tablecloths, and fabric to cover furniture and cushions. Old-fashioned embroidered or lacy hand towels make lovely presents, both traditional and romantic.

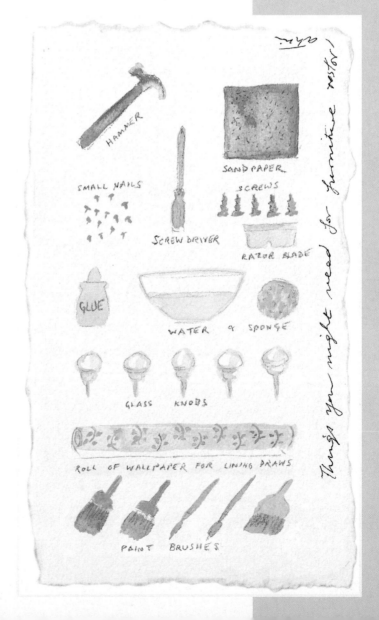

HAMMER

SMALL NAILS

SCREW DRIVER

SAND PAPER

SCREWS

RAZOR BLADE

GLUE

WATER & SPONGE

GLASS KNOBS

ROLL OF WALLPAPER FOR LINING DRAWS

PAINT BRUSHES

Things you might need for furniture restorer!

1

2

3

4

5

6

7

8

9

10

11

12

13

14

15

16

17

18

Loving
Greetings

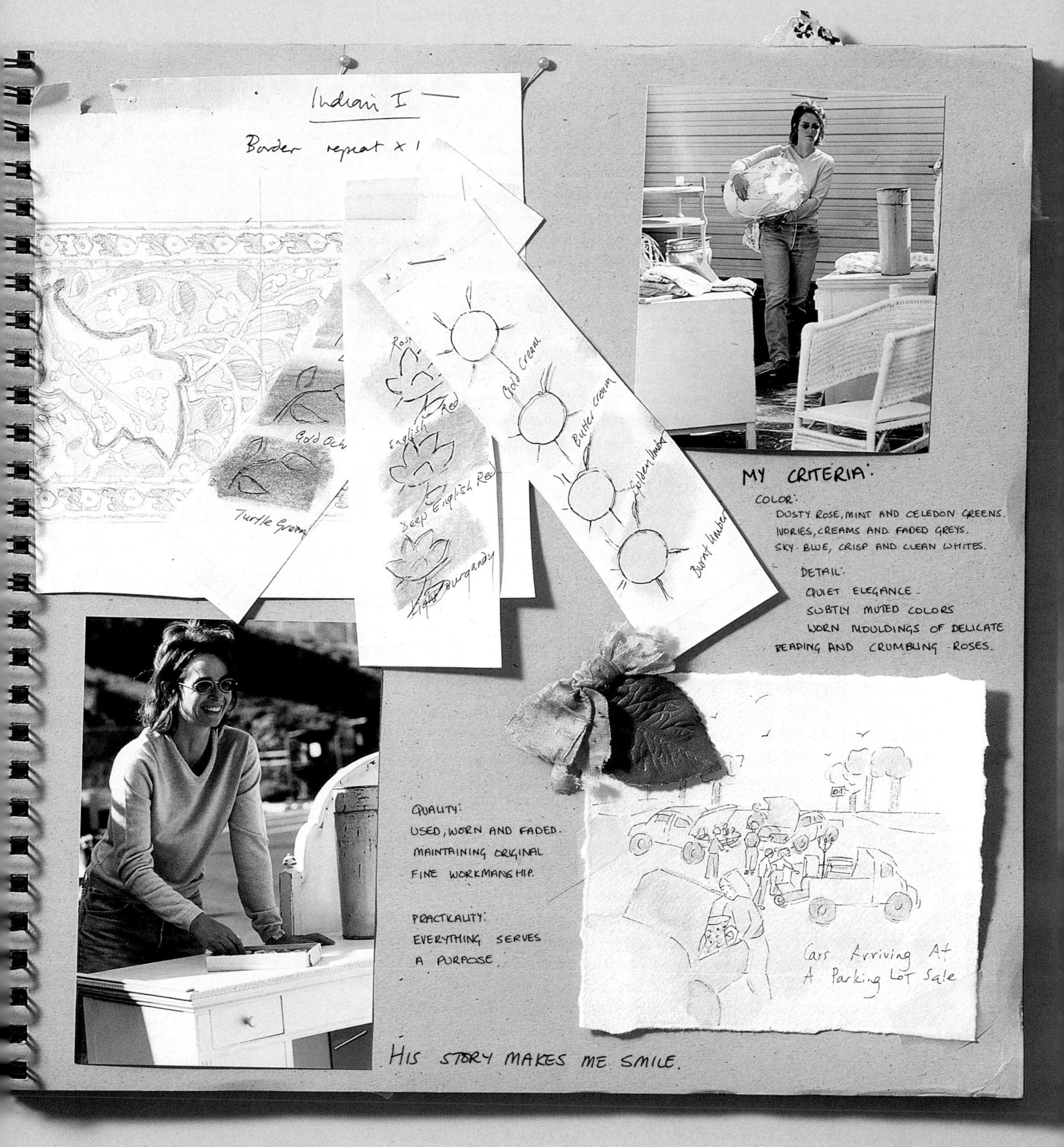

Indian I —

Border repeat x 1

Turtle Green

Gold Och—

Rose
English Red
Deep English Red
Light Burgundy

Gold Cream
Butter Cream
Golden Umber
Burnt Umber

MY CRITERIA:

COLOR:
DUSTY ROSE, MINT AND CELEDON GREENS.
IVORIES, CREAMS AND FADED GREYS.
SKY-BLUE, CRISP AND CLEAN WHITES.

DETAIL:
QUIET ELEGANCE.
SUBTLY MUTED COLORS
WORN MOULDINGS OF DELICATE
PEADING AND CRUMBLING ROSES.

QUALITY:
USED, WORN AND FADED.
MAINTAINING ORIGINAL
FINE WORKMANSHIP.

PRACTICALITY:
EVERYTHING SERVES
A PURPOSE.

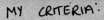

Cars Arriving At
A Parking Lot Sale

HIS STORY MAKES ME SMILE.

Although at first glance this salvaged built-in might seem like it needs professional restoration, the tasks at hand are actually rather simple. (Mark first has to gather his strength and his thoughts).

A simple checklist is created. The contact paper is the first to be removed, by just peeling.

Remove the linoleum (linoleum is a common material to be dealt with in these old built-ins). Peeling, picking, and patience are the tools needed here. Occasionally some of the original top may become vulnerable and bruised. You can glue down the loose ends and lightly sand them to blend the surfaces together. The final coat of paint should act as reinforcement.

If for any reason the glass breaks, remove it carefully. Take exact measurements for a new piece of glass (the thickness depends on the piece), then tack into place with small nails called brads. Before the paint is applied, a thorough cleaning and light sanding is required to remove any loose bits of dust, dirt, or grime. Tape the edge of the glass with masking tape before painting the wood trim. Use primer first to make way for one or two coats of semigloss paint. You can paint the inside and the outside the same color. I usually paint over everything—even the hardware. (Just make sure, once the hardware is dry, you loosen any piece that may have become stuck or jammed.) In the event that some paint lands up on the glass, wait until it dries and scrape it off with a razor blade.

Now completed this built-in finds its home holding endless bits in my daughter's room.

This green wood table was a find at Bountiful. Twelve feet long, it is perfect for a conference. Placing glass on the top creates a smooth writing surface and allows for displaying photos. A wicker chair gets tested with some of my fabric designs.

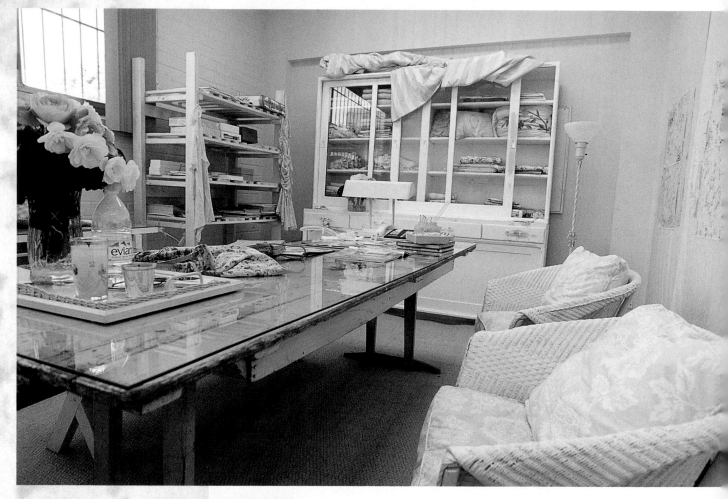

I use this metal desk lamp for additional light—it helps me forget the yucky overhead fluorescent light that came with my office.

A finishing palm sander is used mainly for smoothing surfaces. Use it to lightly skim the top off a painted piece for a bit of distressing, or to smooth wood putty. It allows for more control than the circular sander that would be used for a more drastic task, such as totally stripping off paint from a piece of furniture.

A wonderful mercantile cabinet among the patio furniture stands proudly. It is perfect for a kitchen or an office. With such an expanse of white wood, some glass draw pulls in place of metal handles would offer a sparkle.

White Cabinet

Removed Metal Handles

Patched Holes

The first step would be to remove the holes left by the metal handles. The smoother the application of putty the less sanding is necessary. Two hours of hardening will be required before light sanding is done to smooth out the edges. Drill holes for new glass draw pulls; always make the hole a little smaller than the screw to give some torque. Finally, some simple dusting and cleaning will transform this piece. In this case, no painting was ever needed.

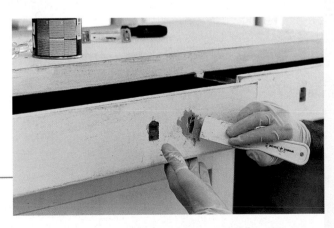

If you find yourself wanting to distress the paint from a piece of furniture, choose your spots intelligently: where there would be natural wear and tear, around draw pulls or knobs, edges, and on top of surfaces.

How lucky I was to find, with a little light sanding, my green under the white.

A filing cabinet is always a nice discovery. Check the ease of the drawer sliding. Large glass knobs will enhance this piece nicely.

Both are structurally sound, so I buy them; the rocker will require a cleaning to make it as good as—or, better than—new. The table does not warrant the expenditure of money or labor; I will cover the top with a piece of washed-out cotton print cloth and a sheet of glass. I pay for them, and as I walk away I make a mental note of some slightly more damaged pieces. One, at least, deserves further consideration.

By now I am thirsty and a little tired. I have had a successful morning and I pause for a drink. Because flea-market food tends to be neither very appetizing nor particularly nutritious, I have brought a sandwich and some fruit from home. While I take my break, I chat with a few vendors I know.

This cabinet, now with glass drawer handles, is the perfect solution to hold all my bits in my office.

This knobless chest of draws had the perfect finish when I found it at the Santa Monica Flea Market. The blue trim on the inside of the draws created a lovely accent waiting to be lined.

Lining the drawers with vintage wallpaper is a wonderful way to complete restoration of a piece.

Now it stands as the foundation for "The Doll House."

The final addition was to add crystal knobs. The unusual proportion of this piece made it appropriate for placement in a tight spot.

225

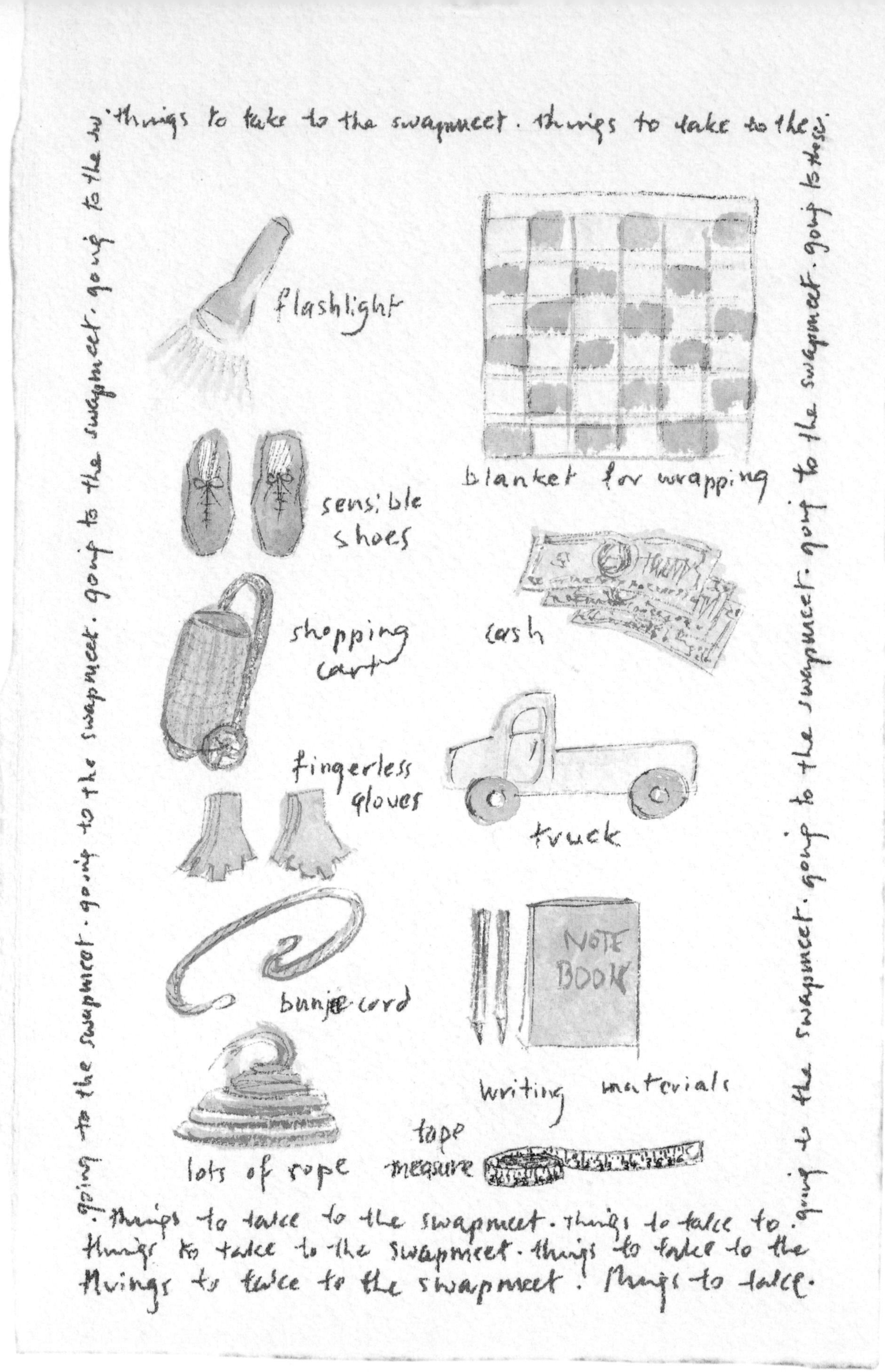
things to take to the swapmeet · things to take to the s
flashlight
blanket for wrapping
sensible shoes
shopping cart
cash
fingerless gloves
truck
bunjee cord
NOTE BOOK
writing materials
tape measure
lots of rope
things to take to the swapmeet · things to take to ·
things to take to the swapmeet · things to take to the
things to take to the swapmeet · things to take ·

I ask one about floral oil paintings—I always have a need for them and love the way the dark cracks in the old oil paint contrasts with the delicate blues, pinks, and greens of the flowers. This dealer doesn't have any but promises to keep an eye open for some. I enjoy these moments of conversation at markets.

This is a good moment to go over my list of what I have bought and what I have spent. This is largely a cash business, so I keep careful accounts. Although I keep one eye open for that once-in-a-lifetime buy, making a fortune from some treasure that only I recognize is a very long shot. Instead, I try to buy items that please my eye for a fair price.

Dishes in blues, greens, deep pinks; sparkling glassware and vases of china or colored and clear glass, dazzling in the sunlight. The glint from the small blue-rib-boned bundles of silver spoons. Decorations—the approach makes me think of fairyland. I take some time to adjust my eye to visualize the uses for the variety of wares in front of me. (Remember, everything must be functional.) I am charmed by a plate with a lavender pattern. I'm not sure I'd want to eat off a lavender plate, but it seems to me that with three or four cakes of pink soap on it, it would look very good in my white-tiled bathroom. I buy it, because it is far from expensive and I have never seen one quite like it.

Happily in possession of the lavender plate, I turn my attention to the glassware. There is still plenty of pressed inexpensive glass—clear, pink, green, amber—in different qualities and weights for sale at flea markets. I buy a selection of pressed glass bowls, which will have many uses—salads, fruit, desserts—and a cream-colored jug with a muted pastel floral design on the front, probably from the late twenties or early thirties. It will be useful either as a serving piece, or, as I visualize it now, full of flowers. It would also make a wonderful present. If a piece of china appeals to me I don't mind if it is slightly chipped—there are many chips and imperfections in this particular fairyland—and a coat of nail polish covers a multitude of defects. There is also a large box of inexpensive decorations. I never waste money on new, store-bought wrapping or ribbon. During the year I pick up a variety of silk flowers, Christmas decorations, and small beaded brooches and store my decorations in a miniature chest of drawers made of stiff cardboard and covered with vintage wallpaper, originally intended for lingerie. My bits and bobs are filed away in the various drawers, and when I need to wrap a present I can easily choose the decoration that seems most fitting for the recipient and the gift.

I tore this myself accidentally—although the painting is pretty, it doesn't warrant expensive restoration. Simple linen tape applied to the back and a light smudging of paint over the tear is an acceptable repair that adds character.

One of the most co[...]
chairs I have eve[...]
this rocker. In its [...]
form it lacked luste[...]
simple task of wra[...]
old but fresh white t[...]
around its seat elev[...]
anoth[...]

Setting off toward vintage clothing, I keep one eye open for frames, particularly if they are oversized (larger than 3' x 4'). I love the theatricality of a huge mirror, the glass mottled enough to add character, but not so mottled that it isn't useful. I often paint the carved wood or gold frame white, because I like the effect to be dramatic, not overwhelming.

Next I visit a booth that sells beds, bedside tables, sofas, chairs, and armoires. None of the beds have the level of carved floral detail that I look for—or the patina, the layering of paint—but I see two armoires I could use. One has lovely little carvings of roses. On the other the molding is incomplete, but there are beautiful details of worn-away wreaths, angels, and a floral design. I like this piece best, partly because the moldings are so worn—if they looked newer they would be too overwhelming. I think the first armoire is over-priced; I make an offer, which the vendor declines, but after a little negotiating I buy the second and continue on my way.

Whether I had an existing need for these fabulous antique French frames, or not, I would always snap them up. Priceless and beautifully detailed moldings in a variety of conditions are a typical example of decayed elegance. Adding mirrors and making sure the frames are bracketed for safe hanging are simple restoration steps to a wonderful piece. Here one sits casually on Liz's floor.

The vintage clothing booths are clustered together. Many of my jeans and cashmere cardigans come from the flea market, and I often buy my dress-up or special-occasion clothes at vintage clothing and textile shows. The silks and satins, the embroideries, and bias-cut dresses reflect a level of detail and workmanship only found today in couture collections.

It is now time for me to collect my purchases. It has been a rewarding and productive morning. Over the years I have learned to go through a flea market quickly, and because most of my visits take place on my Sunday off after a working week, I try to be finished by noon. The flea markets themselves usually close at about three o'clock. I almost always find something. Although occasionally I return home empty-handed, I never feel the day has been wasted, having learned something, enjoyed talking to vendors and friends, and further defined what I like, what is aesthetically important and meaningful to me.

Tired and pleased, I have already collected some of my goods when I catch a glimpse from across two aisles of something cream with a touch of dusty pink. I feel that familiar flutter and, quickening my pace, cut across toward the stall where the possible treasure lies. This reaction, less of a skill than a time-learned instinct, has served me well.

There are many venues where you can look for antiques and second-hand treasures. My favorites are flea markets and antiques malls.

MISCELLANEOUS SIDEBAR INFORMATION

Washing Porcelain

PUT A TOWEL IN THE BOTTOM OF THE SINK AND FILL WITH WARM WATER, NOT HOT, AND A MILD DISHWISHING SOAP TO WHICH YOU HAVE ADDED ONE OUNCE OF CLEAR AMMONIA. SOAK AND RINSE WELL.

Washing Glass

TO CLEAN GLASS, SOAK IN A SOLUTION OF WARM WATER MIXED WITH 1/4 CUP OF CLEAR AMMONIA. RINSE WELL AND DRY CAREFULLY. AS WITH PORCELAIN, IT IS A GOOD IDEA TO PLACE A TOWEL IN THE BOTTOM OF THE SINK FIRST WHEN WASHING DELICATE CRYSTAL. SOME OLD GLASS BOTTLES CAN BECOME CLOUDED OR DISCOLORED AND CAN BE TREATED BY SOAKING IN A MIXTURE OF ONE CUP OF AMMONIA AND FOUR CUPS OF WARM WATER. ANOTHER METHOD IS TO MIX SAND WITH DENATURED ALCOHOL AND SWIRL IT AROUND IN THE CONTAINER UNTIL IT LOOKS CLEAR. WHITE VINEGAR AND WATER MAY BE USED TO SOAK OFF SEDIMENT THAT MAY HAVE ADHERED TO THE INSIDE OF A GLASS CONTAINER. FILL CONTAINER WITH THIS MIXTURE AND LEAVE TO SOAK FOR A FEW DAYS.

Cleaning Brass

CUT A LEMON IN HALF, DIP IT IN SALT AND USE TO SCRUB BRASS. THIS WORKS WELL FOR COPPER TOO. YOU CAN ALSO MAKE A SCRUBBING PASTE FROM ONE TABLESPOON EACH OF SALT, FLOUR, AND WHITE VINEGAR. RUB ON AND BE SURE TO RINSE WELL IN EITHER METHOD.

Removing Rust

USE A WIRE BRUSH TO REMOVE LOOSE RUST FROM WROUGHT IRON FURNITURE AND ORNAMENTS. THEN SAND LIGHTLY OR RUB WITH SOME FINE STEEL WOOL DIPPED IN KEROSENE. AFTER THE KEROSENE HAS DRIED, THE PIECE CAN BE PAINTED WITH AN OUTDOOR PAINT.

Removing Beverage Rings

TO TRY AND REMOVE THOSE WHITE RINGS LEFT ON WOOD SURFACES FORMED BY CONDENSATION FROM DRINKING GLASSES, TRY MIXING UP A PASTE OF CIGARETTE ASH WITH SOME BEESWAX FURNITURE PASTE. RUB ON LIGHTLY AND BUFF WITH A DRY SOFT CLOTH. YOU CAN THEN REWAX THE WHOLE SURFACE IF NECESSARY.

Reviving Cane & Wicker

OLD WICKER OR CANE FURNITURE CAN BE HOSED OFF OUTDOORS TO REMOVE LOOSE DUST AND GRIME. IF NEEDED, IT CAN BE SCRUBBED WITH A SMALL BRUSH DIPPED IN DISHWASHING LIQUID AND WATER. RINSE AND SUN DRY. IT CAN BE VARNISHED IN A MATTE TO GLOSS FINISH OR PAINTED WITH A THIN COAT OF GOOD QUALITY PAINT. FOR SAGGING WOVEN CANE SEATS, COMPLETELY SOAK THE CANING WITH HOT WATER AND LEAVE TO TIGHTEN AND DRY IN THE SUN.

Dying Unfinished Wood

LIGHTLY SAND THE BARE WOOD ITEM AND CAREFULLY DUST OFF. APPLY A SOLUTION OF LIQUID 'RIT' DYE WITH A SPONGE IN CIRCULAR MOTIONS. LET DRY COMPLETELY. THE COLOR WILL BE LIGHTER WHEN DRY, SO REPEAT THE APPLICATION OF DYE TO OBTAIN A RICHER COLOR. YOU MAY WISH TO SEAL THE FINISH WITH A COAT OF VARNISH.

FLEA MARKETS

I find flea markets the most fun and the most challenging places to hunt and gather, because they offer the widest variety of merchandise and are the greatest test of skill, once you understand a few basics and don't take any of it too seriously.

There are hundreds, probably thousands, of flea markets across the country. I've listed my favorites in the back of this book, along with information on how to obtain lists of flea markets in your area. Some are held monthly, others less regularly. If they take place more than once a month, I usually don't bother going; vendors don't have time to buy and restock. If you frequent a flea market, you may build relationships with particular vendors, and in time they will be happy to save items of interest to you.

Most vendors price their items with a little negotiating room, but because they work hard and have to put up with moans, groans, and bargaining, I try to decide what an item is worth to me before I ask the best price. It will be my gauge of whether the asking price is fair. In time, gauging a fair price will become second nature to you. Vendors will usually store your purchases if they are cumbersome or if you want to continue shopping empty-handed, but make clear and descriptive notes of where you've left them. Otherwise, when it's time to gather your finds, you may see hundreds of "small green trees by white vans."

Going to some of the larger flea markets (often those that are quarterly or even yearly) takes a little more organization. If your visit will require an overnight stay, make hotel reservations well in advance. If you are very serious and taking a big truck, make sure that the hotel has adequate parking. You may want to take traveler's checks, because many vendors do not accept out-of-town personal checks and are more willing to negotiate in a cash sale.

Because flea markets are held outdoors, consider the weather and be prepared. Comfortable shoes, a lightweight waterproof poncho, and a hat or sun block can be lifesavers. You can find yourself walking miles and miles at flea markets and for the most part in the United States, the only refreshments on hand are hot dogs, coffee, soda, and doughnuts. I bring something a little more healthful and palatable and am always grateful I have done so.

Among the madness and chaos of the flea markets are some stalls with total organization and vision. In this space, the vendor knows what she has and presents it well. You may not uncover hidden treasures, but bargains and uniqueness are still achieved.

Things I Need

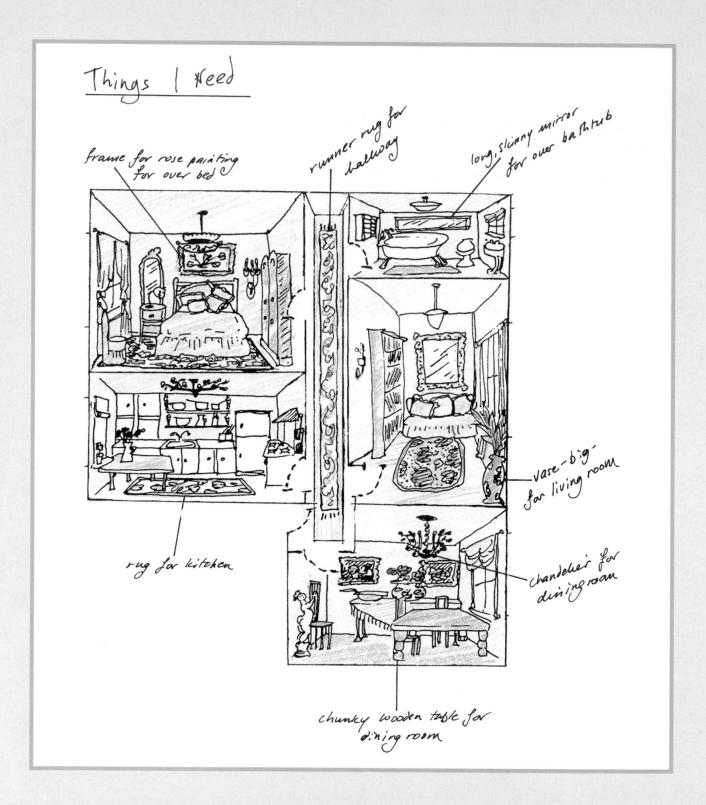

frame for rose painting for over bed

runner rug for hallway

long, skinny mirror for over bathtub

rug for kitchen

vase — big for living room

chandelier for dining room

chunky wooden table for dining room

The most important lesson I have learned during the years, is to be organized and disciplined both practically and emotionally. Knowing what you need or what you like allows for quick thinking. At a flea market, this is half the battle. Showing interest in an item draws attention to it and attracts competitors. If you ponder or dither—you may lose out. The time to buy something is when you first see it. If the price is more than you are prepared to pay, holding out until the end of the day when the vendor may be more amenable to negotiation—is also an option. But it is a risk, too. Being prepared with specifics like measurements and fabric swatches is helpful. Before I understood this, many times I brought home something too large to fit through my door or too small to be of any use.

You will make mistakes; I still do. It happens. I accept my imperfections.

Once I've gathered items, I amaze myself at how loyally I re-create my palette. The little pink mirror's frame will need a small touch-up; all else will need just soap and water.

An Antique Mall

ANTIQUE MALLS

I think antique malls are the best-kept secret and most underrated source of antiques and secondhand goodies.

Nearly every town in the country has an antiques shopping area; the local chamber of commerce can usually tell you where it is located. Within that area there are antiques malls—large buildings, sometimes old warehouses or old barns, that a group of antiques dealers share.

Prices may be a little higher than at flea markets, but this is not always the case and it is such a civilized way to shop. Parking tends to be convenient. Usually each individual booth is not staffed, but wel-coming and cooperative personnel are available to answer questions and help carry goods.

Merchandise is clearly displayed and accessible and I have time to ponder. I rarely feel that an item will be snapped up by somebody else if I don't make up my mind immediately. Some malls will even put things on hold for a few days or offer them on lay-away.

There is usually a 10 percent negotiating margin, although isolated booths within the mall may have their own sales and there significantly larger discounts can be obtained. Most antiques malls will be happy to take checks or credit cards.

As with flea markets, shopping in antiques malls requires imagina-tion and perseverance. I often spend days driving from one mall to another, and I never come home empty-handed.

This very small section of Nina and Lou's compact house is not to be wasted. It serves as a library and office area. The choice of colors for the desk and storage containers cheers what could have been a gloomy corner.

This pink kitchen table did not need much from my imagination. I found it in a store that does a nice job displaying its wares. You may pay a few pennies more but it's worth it.

One of my finds from Summerland Antiques. Already I think I know where some of these will end up.

At Nina and Lou's this now serves as an end table and cupboard.

Possibility for office

lily's room!

My Palette

A broom.
I love that someone took the time
to paint this a pretty pink.

chapter 2
TEXTILES

TEXTILES

Faded Florals and Laundered Linen

Fabrics—scraps of velvet, ribbon, and lace—are among my first flea-market memories. When I was a small child I used to accompany my mother while she searched the booths for remnants of old but fine fabrics. Small quantities, they needed only to be large enough to replace or repair a doll's finery. As soon as I became tall enough to look over the edge of the counter or table, I was fascinated by the drawers full of exquisite colors, delicate silks and satins, creamy laces, and white crochet. My mother would lift a piece and examine it. "This still has a bit of life in it," she'd say.

The textile booths at flea markets or antiques malls still give me pleasure. Whether I am admiring a neat pile of clean, starched, and ironed linen or rummaging though a jumble of tangled cloth, I enjoy this inexpensive and satisfying way of buying fabric.

Sheets, pillowcases, napkins, and hand towels. All are for sale in mass quantities at flea markets. The essential nobility of old, fine, heavy linen only increases with time. Perhaps more than any other item, linen, especially if it bears an embroidered monogram—a bride's initials, the name of a hotel or even that of a railway line—resonates with the past. I look over each piece carefully, worrying less about minor damage than about stains. Small tears can be mended, and for me, a small, exquisite darn, almost as old as the linen itself, only adds to the charm of the piece. But if the dealer has been defeated by a discolored

patch, it is unlikely I will do any better when I get it home.

Unlike some flea-market goods that seem a little surprised to find themselves down on their luck—being offered for sale, secondhand—fine old linen remains serene. It was made to last forever; rather than being thrown away, its function changed. A heavy old linen sheet, with its hand stitching and patiently produced embroidery, might have rested for the first few years of its life in a hope chest or bottom drawer, waiting for the girl who had made it to marry and have a home of her own. When the sheet became worn it would have been carefully mended and, later still, when too threadbare to be repaired, it might be cut down for another use—perhaps a sheet for a child's bed—and eventually would end its days as cleaning rags with years of history. Fine linen evokes elegance, luxury, civility, quality, durability, economy—it is the antithesis of everything we abhor about our disposable, use-it-once-and-throw-it-away society.

(previous spread)
Evocative of the fresh smell of newly laundered, line-dried fabric and of the ceremonies surrounding the hand washing, wind drying, and sun bleaching of household cotton and linen. Wash day, although one of hard work, was a ceremony of a kind—a ceremony honoring both the quality of the cloth and the hand that made it.

This upstairs sitting room in the Dern's house is at the end of Andrea's studio. It is often used as a place for Andrea's paintings to dry. Wicker is the obvious choice for this sun-filled and summery room. I love Andrea's work and now sell her floral paintings in my shop.

Whenever I see them, I buy heavy old linen sheets, hand monogrammed, white-on-white, along with sets of shams, pillowcases, and hand towels, none of which need to match one another to make a bedroom or guest bathroom sophisticated and welcoming. If they are lacy or trimmed with tiny, precious, hidden frills, they can be laundered and dressed up to make the perfect bridal shower gift or house-warming present.

I believe that old and beautiful objects are meant to be used, to become part of life. So I buy linen napkins by the dozen, often the former property of hotels or restaurants. They accompany all meals, even of the baked-beans-on toast variety. Once you accept that linen or cotton napkins do not always need to be ironed, they become an elegant and almost effortless addition to everyday life and cost less than paper napkins. Needless to say, the finer linen and delicate lace I admire is carefully hand washed and gently ironed.

I am always on the lookout for old voile, fine lawn, and linen. I once bought a set of large curtains made out of lovely puckered white cotton inset with panels of handmade lace. I have yards and yards of it folded up. I use it for tablecloths.

The flea market is still an inexpensive place to buy decent-size lengths of fabric. I buy chintz if the colors fit my palette—pale greens, pinks, cream, and white. I like the Victorian floral patterns of chintz but not its shiny quality, so I put it in the washing machine on the hot cycle and after one or two washes it develops a soft, mellow finish—just the way I like it.

This pink sari doubles as my special table-cloth. I also wear it as a skirt. This may seem an unusual choice, but there are no rules about what can and cannot be used for what purpose. The sparkle on this is so lovely.

(opposite page)
Linen napkins and lacy tablecloths are one of those must-have luxuries at my table—constantly in use, with ironing and matching abandoned.

Curtain lengths are an economical way to buy curtains. You have more leeway about the measurements than you may think. If too long, they don't necessarily need to be taken up. Curtains puddling on a wooden floor give a luxurious, sensuous effect. If too short, you can "lengthen" them by using ribbon straps to hang them on the pole. If not quite full enough, they can simply be draped to one side.

But, to apply one of the key tenets of imaginative flea-market thinking, curtain panels need not be used as curtains. Consider them also as a plentiful and inexpensive source of fabric—an old curtain costs a great deal less than a bolt of new material. Would a piece of faded green willow damask enhance your table even if it didn't quite cover every inch of it? If your ultimate use is something smaller than a curtain, imperfections and even stains need not deter you, because you can cut around the unusable bits. Check the panel and measure it to make sure you have enough usable fabric to cover a cushion, window seat, table, or even a smaller window.

If you come across a good-quality piece of fabric in which the print, workmanship, ruffles, frills, or pleating appeal to you, but the color is off, don't be discouraged. If the fabric is substantial, such as heavy curtaining, have it professionally dyed. It requires a vat large enough for the fabric to circulate freely and avoid a mottled effect. Your dry cleaner can probably do it for you. Another option for changing the color or shade of fabric is tea-staining. Simple and effective, the instant aging is natural and convincing—antique rather than no longer new; home dyes are also easy to use and come with uncomplicated instructions. To fade material,

either bleach it chemically or leave it in the sun; bleach is obviously the faster of the two processes. Not only will the colors become paler, but the patterns will become more subdued and sometimes barely visible. The bleach should be applied carefully, diluted with water, and fabric should always be wet before it is bleached. The texture of fabric can be altered—made lighter and less stiff—by repeated washing and by adding a substantial amount of fabric softener.

Andrea's nook is given respect with one of her paintings. A valence made of tea-towel fabric enhances the window without obscuring light.

A guest towel—I see them all the time at flea markets—is pinned up with thumb tacks and acts as a curtain. Nothing fancy is required, since you rarely need to open the curtain on a bathroom window.

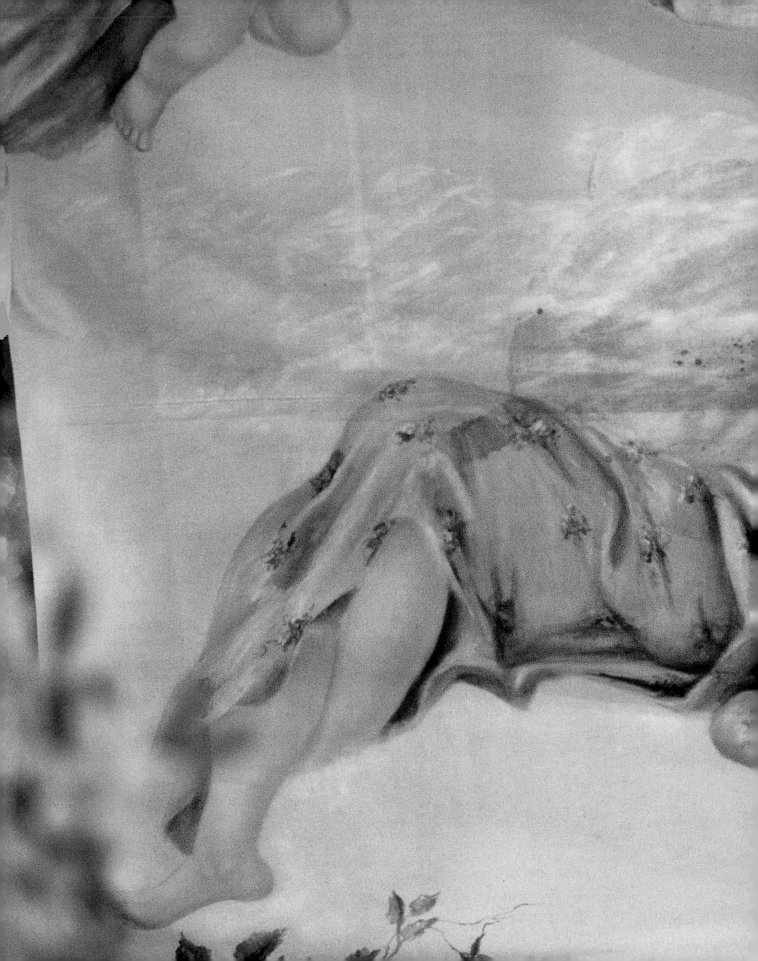

This hand-painted canvas drop cloth—
probably a remnant from a theatrical
project—would be a casual and whimsical
wall covering (no framing necessary).

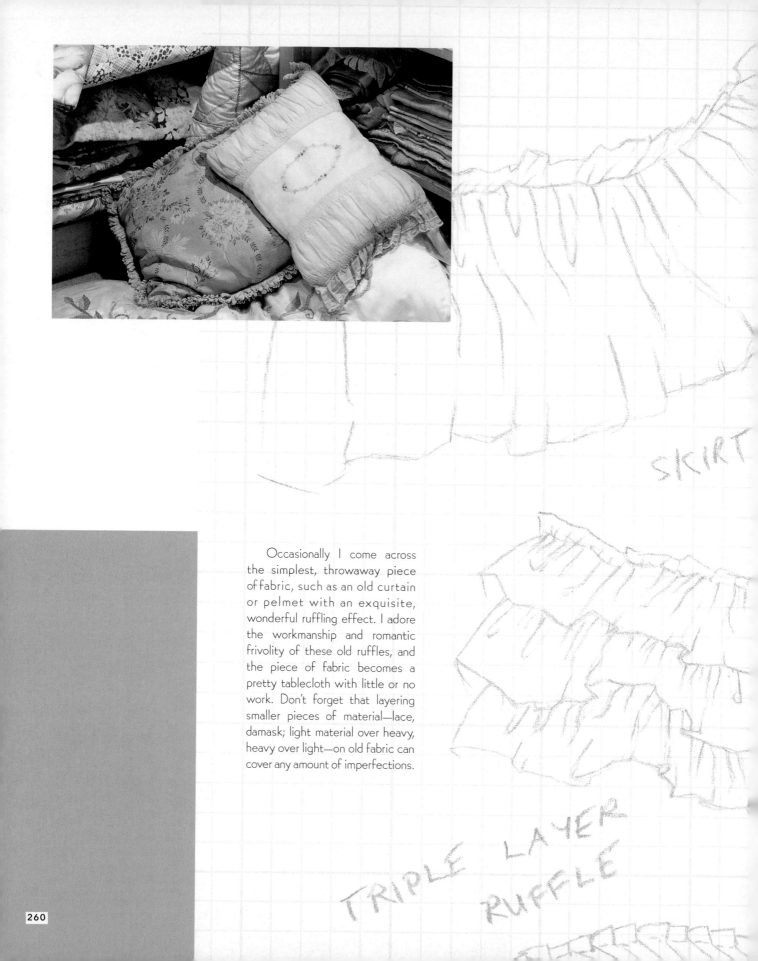

Occasionally I come across the simplest, throwaway piece of fabric, such as an old curtain or pelmet with an exquisite, wonderful ruffling effect. I adore the workmanship and romantic frivolity of these old ruffles, and the piece of fabric becomes a pretty tablecloth with little or no work. Don't forget that layering smaller pieces of material—lace, damask; light material over heavy, heavy over light—on old fabric can cover any amount of imperfections.

SKIRT

TRIPLE LAYER RUFFLE

A pile of lavender fabric at Lorraine Fogwell's store inspired a theme—throw pillows with an assortment of ruffles.

I was fortunate enough to buy ten of these exquisite chairs at Bountiful. They are my favorites, and I scatter them throughout my home. I dress them with or without skirt slips depending on whether I want a fancy or a formal look.

Andrea had many pieces of her furniture covered in this costly fabric, anticipating it would fade. Twelve years later it was still crisp and bright so she decided to fade it herself. She tried a couple of different processes on the fabric sleeves and she ended up using bleach and Rit color removal to achieve an instant, faded elegance.

Andrea and Bruce inherited a pair of these unassuming chairs. The simple little slip allowing the legs to show evokes informality. Fabric sleeves on the arms allow for easy, regular washing of the most used part of the chair.

Fortunately most of Andrea's pieces were slipcovered (for the bleaching process); however, in the case of this upholstered ottoman base, eyes rarely see where the fading process couldn't reach.

Although slipcovers to me are the way to renovate any upholstered piece of furniture, endless washing of certain fabrics may cause shrinkage. Andrea helped the length of this skirt by adding some ribbon trim to the hemline.

Andrea had this inexpensive wicker chair floating around. She applied pink paint and a couple of finely ruffled pillows and ended up with a very unique and appealing piece.

Wicker of various qualities is still relatively easy to come by. It's a wonderful casual addition either inside or out. To avoid the expense of reupholstering, laying and tucking an old quilt as Andrea has done complements the wicker perfectly.

Andrea and Bruce inherited this comfy and friendly chair and footstool. Andrea opted not to slipcover this piece, but by simply whitewashing the legs with Gesso, she gave their chair a youthful feel.

Blankets are useful scattered about. This one has nice layering and a lovely texture. A throwaway but subtle detail.

More perhaps than any other commodity, fabric—with a little thought and not much more expense—can dramatically affect the look and atmosphere of a room, making it sophisticated, soft, sensuous, welcoming, and luxurious.

Chairs and sofas may be transformed by slipcovers—from the soft warmth of velvet in winter to the cool pale greens and dusty roses of summer, and from the grandeur of damask to the simplicity of modern, functional white denim. However, you don't necessarily need to go to the trouble or expense of slipcovers. A length of fabric draped over a piece of furniture can change the whole mood of a room. Andrea Dern, for instance, uses her white crocheted bedcover to transform a tired sofa.

An old-fashioned formal dining-room table can become soft and romantic with a candle-lit crocheted lace cloth—or cool and welcoming for a summer lunch with a washed-out cotton floral print, evocative of the fresh smell of newly laundered, line-dried fabric, and of the ceremonies surrounding the hand-washing, wind-drying, sun-bleaching of household cotton and linen. Wash day, although hard work, was a ceremony of a kind, honoring both the quality of the cloth and the hand that made it.

An average, unexciting plastic patio chair becomes a thing of beauty by disguising the cushion with some lovely fabric.

Andrea covered this sofa in a Ralph Lauren sheet sewn inside out (inside out for more subtle color, a sheet for less cost than yardage).

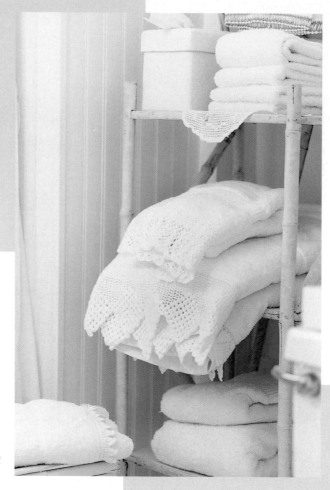

While on her
husband's movie
sets, Andrea lends
her talents to
crocheting lace
borders, which she
then applies to
plain towels. (For
those unable to
crochet, pieces of
lace and crochet
are easily found
and can be attached
in this manner.)

Boxes and boxes
of lace and crochet,
waiting to be
rummaged through,
can be used in their
original forms or
can be applied to
other items.

Draping a bedspread over a tired sofa is the simplest way to transform it, as Andrea did in her spare room.

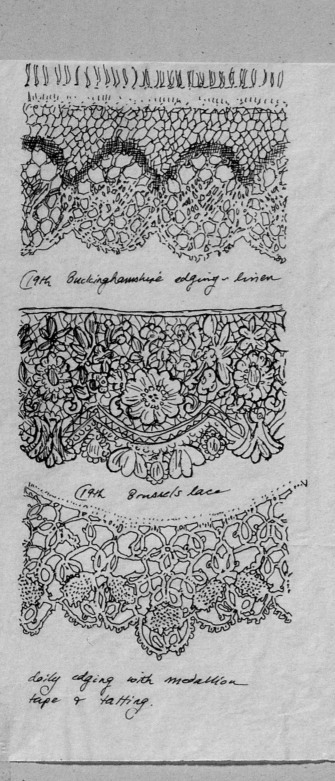

C19th Buckinghamshire edging - linen

C19th Brussels lace

doily edging with medallion tape & tatting.

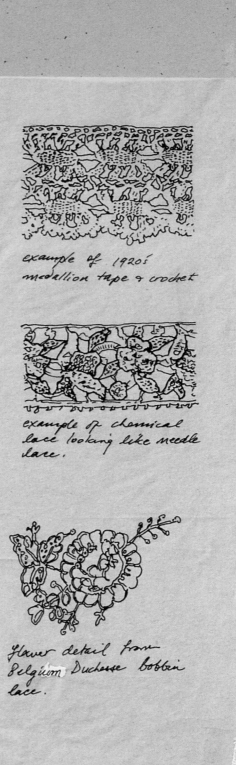

example of 1920's medallion tape & crochet

example of chemical lace looking like needle lace.

Flower detail from Belgium Duchesse bobbin lace.

CASTLES IN THE SAND

Playful words brings a smile to my
face in memory of childhood.

chapter 3

COLLECTIONS
& ODDITIES

COLLECTIONS & ODDITIES
The Recognized Object

When you shop at a flea market you are on your own, without the reassurance that comes with the advertised, mass-produced purchase, accompanied by an illustration on the package showing you how to use it and

M. L. Peacor collects with a rhyme, reason, and method. Even common stones are gathered with an eye for their subtle tone and worn texture. Soothing to look at, calming to touch.

where to put it. At the flea market, your own taste is your only guide—uninfluenced by what is currently being pushed in the shop windows and mail-order catalogues. Here you can express yourself in how you furnish your home, the clothes you wear, or the presents you give.

Objects that no longer work for their intended purpose can often be used for another. Allow yourself to be open to possibilities. If I see something I really like but don't know what to do with it, I pick it up, hold it, and after a while, I know or sense how I can use it. Some things take a little longer than others. I looked at a box of old, amber, slightly irregular glass chandelier drops for a long time before I saw a cache of paper weights and single-bar soap dishes...and many small original presents. Flea markets and antiques malls are full of objects that are either obsolete or damaged, unable to perform their original function. Many, like my chandelier drops, are tiny, while others are quite large. Andrea Dern was charmed by a wheeled wicker marketing basket. Its wheels no longer roll easily, but she has painted it cream, lined it with an everyday trash bag, and keeps it in her kitchen, wheeling it around from one work surface to another to collect trash .

If you bake and decorate cakes, a pressed glass pedestal cake stand with a sterling silver base is a welcome find. But even if you don't know where your kitchen is located, don't pass by too quickly. Visualize it in the bathroom, perhaps displaying half a dozen cakes of soap in neutral tones. Or a large, plain white pottery bowl, perhaps originally intended for serving mashed potatoes to a family of eight, can be beautiful on a coffee table in a studio apartment, filled with smooth gray and green pebbles—tactile and pleasing to hold.

Although the wheels on this shopping trolley no longer stand up to street use, Andrea cleverly uses it in her kitchen to collect trash from different workspaces.

(previous spread)
It is easy to find cake plates similar to this one at flea market or antiques malls. This is perfect in my bathroom holding a few items I wanted separated from my array of toiletries.

*This common pearlized shell
provides a nest to store these soaps.*

A marble scalloped platter makes for a handsome display.

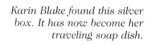

Karin Blake found this silver box. It has now become her traveling soap dish.

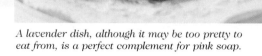

A lavender dish, although it may be too pretty to eat from, is a perfect complement for pink soap.

A plain white food dish!

I uncovered a box of decorative glass drops from an oversized chandelier. One can be a spot for soap, another a paperweight. One for me and plenty more for gifts?

Sometimes an object that doesn't stand out on its own makes a better impression as one of a set, a concept rather than an accident. For example, a well-designed but far from delicate woven wire or metal basket—even one large and solid enough to have contained outdoor garbage—will fit in pleasantly indoors if it is one of several painted the same color. Maybe unexpectedly pink? Or lined with white linen or

denim? Small antique bottles and kitchen jars are ideal for small flower arrangements and make thoughtful and inexpensive presents.

Although I view collecting as a suspect habit, developing a theme, particularly around a color, can be a highly effective decorating device. Sue Balmforth has shelves of yellow, green, and cream pottery—each piece pretty in itself, but the effect of the whole collection is greater than the sum of its parts.

Another exception to my antipathy toward collecting is Andrea Dern's use of small, individual pieces of crockery—restaurant or hotel creamers and butter plates—for entertaining. When she gives tea or dinner parties, each guest has his own tiny creamer and a plate just the right size for three pats of butter in front of his place setting.

I was charmed by these pink waste bins in the bathroom of a Beverly Hills club—a gentle reminder to me that I can always paint a common item in the most subtle way.

279

A wicker hamper can double as a side table and hide laundry as Andrea has done here.

While walking through flea markets and tag sales, I keep one eye open for aesthetically pleasing storage, ranging from Karin Blake's small silver box, used as a traveling soap dish, to a creaky, old-fashioned, wicker laundry basket in which large objects can be stored.

This is as good a moment as any to mention one of my basic beliefs pertaining to the functionally organized and visually pleasing home: Less is more. Storage should not be a way of keeping unsightly junk out of sight. I don't like the idea of my house being full of things I don't need, so what I do have deserves decent storage. It gives me a sense of calm order when I open a cupboard and find its contents in neat and logical order. I divide the things I store into three rough categories. If the item in my hand doesn't fit into one of them, I give serious thought to adding it to the recycling bin.

The first category is things you use every day—in the kitchen, bathroom, office, or closet. Be it an antique saucer for paper clips or a metal tin to hold socks, the storage container should be functional—an antique box, for instance—of the right size and pleasing to the eye. If architectural excellence or location is more important to you than square footage, you might consider the choices made by Nina and Lou and by M.L., who have made their storage containers attractive enough in color, proportion, and shape to contribute to their decor.

Nina and Lou—Nina is responsible for the lovely flower arrangements in my shop—live in a little house (450 square feet). Common sense and taste have gone a long way to solve this house's main problem, which is, of course, space. Much of the charm of this house comes from the ingenuity with which they have incorporated storage into the overall decor. Accessible and attractive storage (not stuffed and crammed) is easily accomplished with a collection of interesting containers, using them in ways other than originally intended. Their home is functional, hence balanced and beautiful.

A wire shopping basket, lined, holds some of Lou and Nina's linens.

This green metal tin can could hold a variety of items. Here it holds socks.

Work in progress at Andrea's—a watercolor sketch hangs below her hat-boxes. The boxes provide storage space and are always useful for holding gifts instead of using giftwrap.

A sturdy hatbox becomes a foot rest under Nina's desk, as well as more storage.

The second category requires legitimate long-term or seasonal storage—larger, practically shaped containers for those tax returns and checkbook stubs you don't use but dare not throw away; a painted box for the Christmas tree ornaments; an antique trunk that doubles as a coffee table, where seasonal clothing may be packed away.

Finally, there is the "keep forever" box or drawer where you store the record and treasures of your life—love letters and milk teeth, your children's art and your grandfather's medals, a wedding invitation, postcards from camp. Nostalgia, souvenirs. These deserve a safe, special, and beautiful storage place—a hatbox, perhaps.

The perfect green metal trunk contains important paperwork behind Nina's desk.

Andrea and Bruce's bathroom has the feeling of a greenhouse. In this moist air her flowers thrive.
This green box is home to a mixture of her scent bottles.

The perfect container for the simple toilet roll.

M.L.'s son found one of these frogs in an expensive store—he begged his mom to buy it just to put stuff in it. She was then inspired to pick up another for pennies at a church sale.

Sue Balmforth will never pass up a wire basket. These are from the '20s, '30s, '40s, and '50s. Placed throughout the house, these evoke an interesting theme. They have a variety of uses— storage, waste, laundry.

Sue Balmforth builds collections as she finds these inexpensive pottery pieces. Grouping like colors makes a statement.

Andrea has gathered these creamers on her travels. When she has tea or dinner parties each guest has his or her own jug. Special!

M.L.'s pottery jar collection holds the various tools of her trade. The economical use of space in her home always leaves these items visible. Hence the attractive and practical display.

Petite butter dishes—one for each guest—at Andrea and Bruce's beach house. Only a couple inches in diameter, these tiny plates lend a lovely formality to an informal setting.

Since the stuff for sale at flea markets and antiques malls is usually one-of-a-kind secondhand or antiques, chances are you will not see your findings anywhere else. That is why it is so important to define your taste and develop your eye—to know what you like and to recognize it when you see it.

Less really is more.

TABLETOPS
Chapter 4

TABLETOPS
Informal Elegance and Graceful Nothingness

At M.L.'s house a found olive jar is to me an earthly elegance.

One of my favorite flea-market buys is a turn-of-the-century flowered porcelain bowl with a dull silver rim and base. The ceramic has, over the years, developed a slight crackle—not to be confused with "cracks." I never buy a bowl that is cracked, because it is unhygienic for food and impractical as a flower vase. I love the subdued tones, the tomato red of the design, and its low graceful shape. I use it for flowers—soft white floppy flowers with gray-green foliage give a pleasing "blowsy" effect. Even if the theoretical focal point of your living room is a sofa or mantelpiece, a vase of flowers carefully placed on a tabletop is sure to draw the eye. The same is true of the sparkle and twinkle of a cut-glass bowl. Such simple and unpretentious details add character and personality to a room.

Your table will most clearly reflect your taste if you place on it only what you actually need. Just be sure those objects are functional and beautiful. A table that holds an antique glass lamp, a bunch of flowers in a flea-market olive jar, and a book has no need for ornaments or frou-frou.

An old milk bottle stands with an unevenly painted vase. It's pretty enough with or without flowers as a tabletop display.

(on previous spread)
Such a therapeutic task—warm sudsy water, ending with satisfaction of a job well completed.

I'm not quite sure how this porcelain and silver-trimmed bowl was originally used. I've found it's perfect for flowers, allowing them to wilt gently.

A jug decorated with lemons is lovely for these free-form roses.

A vase with a life of its own. The depth of texture and color of this piece caught my eye as I paced through the flea markets. Tiny chips here and there were camouflaged with nail polish.

M.L. put a lovely display of Gerber daisies in this pot.

A table needs little more than a beautiful vase of flowers. This is a typical example of a flea-market–found vase. I love Nina's flower arrangements.

Nina and Lou's tiny kitchen is humble but beautifully practical. Dainty curtains replace cumbersome cupboard doors. A chopping block covers what was once an extra sink. The draining board is a safe resting place for an eclectic collection of old one-off dishes.

Sue adds delicacy by tying a fresh rose with twine to an unironed flea-market linen napkin. I love them.

(opposite page)
For weddings, birthdays, and all festive occasions there is not a prettier table than one arranged by Sue Balmforth. Here she mixes sturdy inexpensive restaurant seconds with English and French, delicate red, white, and pink glasses. The combination is perfect.

In the kitchen and the bathroom, I try to dispense with the extraneous and present and store what remains in as clean and simple a manner as I can. An antique porcelain dish on a white- tiled surface. An old glass scent bottle used as a bud vase.

The table at which you eat and about which family conversations take place can be greatly enhanced by what you bring back from the flea market. Whether you are feeding the children a spaghetti supper on hotel monogrammed white soup plates, pouring their milk into mismatched thirties milk-glass tumblers, and encouraging them to wipe their fingers on unironed and slightly worn cotton napkins; or setting the table for a festive Thanksgiving dinner, there is plenty of room for inexpensive creativity and imagination. The special occasions, weddings, birthdays, holidays, or dinner parties are occasions when family silver, heirloom wineglasses, or the pearl-handled fruit knives you inherited from your great-grandmother can be advantageously mingled with flea-market finds. This adds a sense of your own taste and imagination while ensuring enough serving dishes. Again, objects do not need to serve their original purposes. Sometimes extravagance and luxury is conveyed by using something grand for a more pedestrian purpose. Karin Blake uses blue and white flow-ware soup tureens—complete with lids and set on platters—as individual soup bowls, adding a touch of elegance and formality to the meal. Needless to say, the tureens do not need to match one another, although a similar or sympathetic color and approximately equal sizes helps.

A mixture of elegance, informality, and beauty—as in old silver, a worn napkin, and a fresh flower—can add grace to a dinner table and is infinitely preferable to the perfectly matched, pristine newness of settings sold by stores whose names are synonymous with luxury and high prices.

Milk glass is a sturdy, nicely detailed addition to any place setting.

(opposite page) Elegance needn't be lost with children's dinners of compulsory pasta. A chandelier from Bountiful sets the mood; the framed mirror was a keeper once I got it home from Santa Monica Flea Market. The purely decorative pastel painting reflects my palette perfectly. Sturdy milk glass and mismatched linens allow for heavy-handed sticky fingers.

These nothing metal jugs became something with flowers and the commitment to creating a collection.

Pressed glass is a very acceptable substitute for crystal and easy to find. Once again, the abundance is the statement.

(opposite page) Presenting each guest with their own individual pressed-glass bud vase at the dinner table is elegance on a budget. It can be your secret.

Even more than the dining-room table, the kitchen offers creative opportunities for using pretty and original flea-market treasure. The heavy earthenware jars that once held marmalade or peanut butter make pleasing containers for kitchen implements or may be used to store or even serve food. Old glass—bowls, glasses, cups, and saucers of pressed, plain, colored, or milk glass—is still easy to find at flea markets. It is so useful: as a substitute for fragile and expensive crystal; to display a bouquet of flowers; to store pens and pencils on the desktop or beside the telephone; or to hold toothbrushes and make-up brushes.

Every so often, I take everything off the tabletop, and give the ruffled, washed-out chintz a good shake. I feel as though I am not just getting rid of dust and wrinkles but bringing it back to life. When I put the objects back on the tabletop—the vase of fresh flowers, the newly dusted lamp, the small pile of books—the subtle alteration in their placement gives the objects a new life. This seems to prevent the "dead" feeling that pervades a room that, although perfectly clean, is not lived in. Because every object I move is one I have carefully chosen and thoughtfully placed, this activity is more a pleasure than a chore.

FLOW WARE

Flow ware is blue china: English, old, and gloriously imperfect. Before glazing was perfected, the blue patterns made by Staffordshire potters tended to bleed. Today these pieces, each slightly different, are both prized and collected—and a little harder to find.

KARIN BLAKE

"I am always rummaging through funny little shops," Karin Blake says. She is a decorator and collects primitive furniture and folk art. She comes from New England and now lives in Malibu. Her design sense is one of puritan elegance. Although her taste might seem to be aesthetically in conflict with Shabby Chic, it is surprising how often we admire the same look or are pleased by the same idea or object—her blue-and-white flow-ware mix-and-match dinner service, for instance. She has no inhibitions about combining flea-market and church-sale finds with more serious purchases from a crème-de-la-crème antiques shop. I like that.

She likes "the freedom of white." During her process of designing, she says, "I live in a space and wait. Some solutions are obvious, others emerge with time."

Karin Blake created this elegantly welcoming table. Over the years she has traveled from coast to coast, from churchyard sales to flea markets purchasing blue-and-white flow ware. She uses platters and terrines for individual plates and soup dishes, creating a sense of grandeur for each guest.

Mennecy-Villeroy Vase

Plymouth Covered Garniture Jar

Worcester Chocolate Pot With Domed Lid

Lowestoft Butter Boat

Wedgewood Ivy Pattern Plate

Wedgewood Ivy Pattern Bouillon Cup

Karin collects simple classic stoneware. So use-fully functional, the quantity is the statement.

Peanut butter barrels:
Karin has collected many; these
two are in use in her kitchen.

This lovely cutlery was passed down to Karen from her grandmother—nicely complementing her collection of napkin holders, which holds her varied collection of linen.

Karin treats her linens with the respect age and delicacy deserve. They are laundered, laid on cardboard, tied with a ribbon, and plastic-wrapped. Karin can accept the original stains as the character of age.

Simple, simple, simple—a clear cut-glass lamp with a white linen shade quietly enhances any room.

Andrea picked up this smiling chap on her journeys. Cheerful whimsy. The shade's lining was so tattered that she simply removed it.

Andrea found this at Shabby Chic— another example of inspiration from her garden. A simple parchment shade is all this intricate lamp base needs.

A cool alabaster lamp—rewiring is all I had to do. In the realm of Shabby Chic this will complement any setting.

*Although a little harder to come by than in the past,
this Italian, delicately hand-painted chandelier is a
charming addition to Nina and Lou's house.*

Because I live at the beach, shells have become my natural decoration. My son loved this one, and I made it into a lamp by having an electrician wire it.

DRIFTING

Am I drifting? Am I focused?
Either answer is fine, just
so long as I'm aware.

DECORATIONS
chapter 5

DECORATIONS
The Thought That Counts

The celebration of an event is an acknowledgment of the importance of that event—wedding, christening, birthday, Thanksgiving, or Christmas— and the place it occupies in our lives. Celebration and ritual allow us to express our feelings of love, joy, and gratitude. The ceremony, the tradition, and the decorations and trappings are visible, tangible expressions of how we feel. They help us all to feel the same emotion at the same time. Afterward they become memories, and the decorations can become souvenirs, helping us to recall the emotions and the importance of an event.

(opposite page)
M.L. started her collection of mercury glass decorations with a couple of pieces from an expensive store. She later learned that by buying easily found old, brightly colored ornaments and gently washing and rubbing them in soapy water, she could transform them into pure silver mercury glass. As a final touch, she adds a plain gray ribbon. For Christmas M.L. hangs the smaller mercury balls on a topiary plant, which then becomes her Christmas tree.

I don't think these muted pastel Christmas ornaments could be any prettier.

(previous spread)
I found this multitiered papier-mâché wedding cake and didn't know what use I would find for it, but I knew I definitely had to have it. Since then it has been a dramatic yet welcoming entrance to two weddings. Both times I've draped it with fresh flowers, usually keeping the color monochromatic —cream on cream.

How we decorate is an expression of our individual style. Behind most decorating, for me, is thought, patience, imagination, and the satisfaction of making something that expresses love and affection. The wrapping of presents is a transitory form of decoration and allows me to give free rein to my creative imagination.

Some time ago I bought a very large papier-mâché three-tiered wedding cake and have used it to adorn the entrance to two weddings, decorating the cake with fresh flowers—in one pale color only—to make a festive combination of old and new. The wedding cake was a once-in-a-lifetime find, but there are some decorative items I come upon over and over again. The pale pink sleigh and creamy-toned reindeer—as special as I think it—is a common sight on my travels. Made of flaky wood, it is a warm and evocative respite from the garish colored neon and plastic decorations sold by the less distinguished of our chain stores.

Remnants of a shower. The workmanship is extraordinary.

(opposite page)
A creamy tissue bell with pink silk ribbons found
in a box of like items. I was so attracted by
the yummy color. An elegant subtle decoration
for a shower or wedding.

These delicate velvet fruits were salvaged from the trim of a mirror.

These tiny beaded things I found at the Long Beach Flea Market.

Milliner's decorations I found at Lorraine Fogwell's store. They could be a gift in themselves, but I will use them as gift wrapping trim.

There would be little pleasure for me in spending a lot of money on mass-produced wrapping paper and ribbon to wrap and decorate the presents I give to those I love. I like the outward appearance of each gift to reflect some aspect of my taste, the taste of the person to whom I am giving the present, and possibly to contain a reference to the gift itself.

For me there is something a little sad about the gift-wrapped present sent directly from a department store or mail-order depot. I usually wrap a present in layers of pastel tissue or plain parcel paper or in an antique box. Then I decorate the parcel, either with old ribbon from the flea market or ribbons I tear from strips of plain muslin. I like to finish by adding some little one-of-a-kind decoration I have found on my travels: velvet strawberries from a discarded mirror; silver hat beading from a milliner's oddment box; silk or paper flowers; shells. I think the giving and receiving of a present should be a personal and pleasurable experience. The very effort and thought that goes into finding the decoration is reflected in the result and makes it beautiful.

Simple scallop shells are delicately decorated before they become decorations themselves.

Don't pass up limp or mashed up silk flowers and ribbons. Wave them over the spout of a boiling teakettle, and they will revive and pop back to life. (The steam will be very hot, so use tongs or a potholder.)

*Paper wedding flowers
with silk ribbon crying out
to be recycled—again.*

Flea markets and antiques malls offer a wealth of ribbon, shells, vintage silk, old boxes, and paper flowers. These can be used as you find them, or little knickknacks can be adapted for the decoration. If you look carefully you will find complete collections of decorations left over from parties or functions. Because these are often sold as job lots, by the boxful, you may find you have an additional jumble of assorted cards and decorations. Even if you end up throwing some of these away, you will still have made a good buy and saved money.

*Silk and linen flowers often get passed by. Get into the habit of
buying them. There is always use for them—as a gift, on a hat, or
for decoration.*

I store my spare decorations in a pretty little chest of drawers, similar to the one in which I keep my "keep forever" treasures. The little drawers keep the buttons, bows, flowers, shells, and ribbons separate. The miniature drawer knobs and the antique wallpaper finish remind me of the pleasures of original and creative decoration.

*Whimsy off the beach and a leftover
from something—somewhere.*

*(opposite page)
Adding bits and bobs to packages wrapped in plain
white parcel paper or in fabric remnants creates a
wonderful vision and thought for a gift.*

Humility

 HUMILITY is perpetual quietness of heart. It is to have no trouble. It is never to be fretted or vexed, irritable or sore, to wonder at nothing that is done to me, to feel nothing done against me. It is to be at rest when nobody praises me, and when I am blamed or despised; it is to have a blessed home in myself where I can go in and shut the door and kneel to my Father in secret and be at peace, as in a deep sea of calmness, when all around and about is trouble.

Words I aspire to.

chapter 6
APPAREL 6

APPAREL
Couture, Cashmere, and Camisoles

When I was a child, my sister Deborah, who always had artistic talents, collected antique clothes. She had a basket full of Victorian underskirts, Edwardian high-necked blouses, elegant tea-gowns, and glamorous evening dresses. On Sunday afternoons she would dress up in her finery. At the time I was not much interested, probably because she was my big sister. Later, as an adult designing costumes for commercials in England, I found that my appreciation of the old and the beautifully made grew; soon I was only interested in working on period productions. Choosing and designing contemporary clothes didn't interest me; I was most happy when researching period costumes and rummaging through baskets of old fabrics to find the right trim. I appreciated the romance of ruffles, draping, and extravagant touches. Although I no longer design costumes for commercials, it is a rare day that I do not wear something I bought at a flea market or, to an evening dress-up occasion, a vintage dress show.

PROM DRESSES
fancy dresses

(opposite page)
*Prom dresses found at the
Pickwick Vintage Textile Show:*
- *pale pink*
- *pale green*
- *muted pastels*

*—lovingly handsewn. Chances
are, as prom dresses, they only
have been worn once before
and are begging to be worn again.*

(previous spread)
*The translucent tulle of
these prom dresses evokes
an untouchable femininity.*

fancy dresses

The hang of this fabric, the draping of the train
and the delicacy of the detail (all hand done)
create a work of art in a dress. No fabric was
spared, and it wears beautifully.

circa
1930

333

original

tea stained

bleached

cold-water dyed.

This dress has such potential.
Hemline can be altered
Color can be changed.

Rose pink

My flea-market buys blend with the newer clothes in my wardrobe. I believe flea-market clothing should be worn unselfconsciously and not as a way of re-creating the past. I think of it instead as an opportunity to wear clothes of really lovely quality not available today or, if available, too expensive for everyday use.

It is the mixture of periods and styles that achieve the look I like and in which I feel most comfortable. I buy most of my jeans at flea markets and often wear them with a cashmere sweater. If I had spent five hundred dollars for new cashmere, it would spend most of its time between sheets of tissue paper in a drawer, but my ten- or fifteen-dollar cashmere cardigan gives me a luxurious feeling while I work, relax, or play with my children. Like nearly everything I buy at the flea market, my clothes are for living in—not for fancy dress, not for once-in-a-great-while occasions. My possessions are meant to be used, to be part of my and my children's lives, and to affirm a way of living that is free, comfortable, and aesthetically pleasing.

SWEATERS

Cashmere is an affordable luxury. Vintage-clothing stores and flea markets are places to look, but do check for moth holes. Jeanne, who works in my shop, has an enviable collection of cashmere pullovers and cardigans. I have been fooled many times by the gorgeous quality of sweaters she has bought for pennies.

Once vintage apparel was thought of as secondhand clothes, the very words evoking the image of smelly, torn hand-me-downs. If you were brave and lucky, you might find buttons or scraps of lace to use elsewhere. Today, vintage clothing may be found on the racks not only of flea markets and the Salvation Army but of fashionable main-street boutiques and even auction houses. Some of the specialized vintage-clothing shows or fancier shops offer "dead stock"—vintage clothing that has never been worn. These clothes, as you would expect, cost a little more. Another treasure of the elite vintage circles are European designer suits with the original label intact; the women who bought these expensive clothes in Paris or London often cut the labels out in order to smuggle them through U.S. customs.

This delicate camisole is a wonderful accent, for the innocent detail of hand workmanship. Someone cared enough to make this.

(opposite page) Often available in blue, white, black, and pink, these cardigans add interest to jeans and a tee-shirt or are elegant enough to finish off an evening outfit.

FLORAL PRINTS

A pink velvet bow nestled among a cluster of pink petals makes for such a fun and pretty hat.

The intricacy of these miniature gathers and pleats among the lavender rayon dress is a detail rarely found in the casual dresses of today.

The generous cut of this dress, combined with the faded floral print on fine voile, makes an innocent, simple, pretty summer frock.

Vintage apparel makes even more sense for those once-in-a-lifetime occasions than for day-to-day wear. A wedding gown or prom dress is the most expensive garment you will ever buy, if you calculate its cost against the number of times it is worn. We live in a time when our more formal and festive clothes are only worn occasionally. It's been a long time since anyone I know wore an evening dress until it became threadbare or frayed. The irony is that a vintage dress will be useful and attractive for years to come while this season's model, costing ten times as much, may seem a little dated by this time next year. The vintage gown may even become an heirloom. And I love the feel of vintage handmade clothes, the sense of once-extravagant couture or a simple day dress lovingly crafted by a mother for her daughter.

FLORAL

Detail of
sleeve with
smocking

Although simplicity is the place to start, the qualities of this embroidery
and smocking contributes to the specialness of this top.

PRINTS

The frivolous ruffles and the perfect fading of the print (from endless washing) makes this one of my most favorite and most worn flea-market finds.

The throwaway look of a summer slip dress from the '40s. The fine lawn fabric, the stunning print—little else is needed.

DRESSES

The choice and range of garments for sale at the flea market seems endless—quantities of rayon floral dresses, Victorian undershirts, silk nightdresses, my favorite pastel cashmere cardigans, and perfectly faded Levis. A pair of these Levis with a pale blue cashmere cardigan and a hand-embroidered white-on-white camisole, worn with a belt and shoes from one of today's designers, makes an elegantly casual, useful, and inexpensive outfit. On a warm summer day I like to wear a vintage floral nightie as a dress. Because it is a floral print (washed-out pinks and reds on an off-white background) and made of rayon, it looks and feels like a summer dress. However, if it looked like a nightie—a solid pastel, silky and lacy—no matter how pretty, I would not choose to wear it as a dress, out in public.

Rarely are affordable clothes cut on the bias today. This type of tailoring using the broadest expanse of fabric is more apt to be found in high-end designer lines. (Panels cut and pieced together are more economical). This is a 1940s floral print nightie, which was commonly cut on the bias, creating a sexy flattering silhouette. Found abundantly in silky solid pinks and creams, they remain lovely nightgowns. This being patterned, however, adapts beautifully as a day dress.

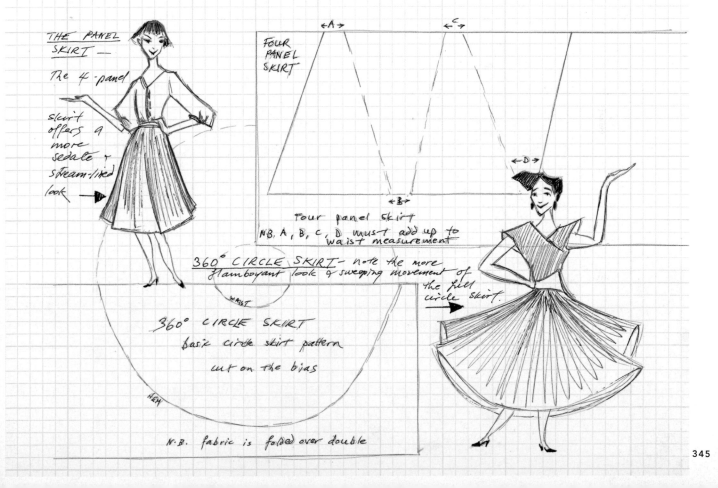

THE PANEL SKIRT —

The 4-panel skirt offers a more sedate & stream-lined look ➤

FOUR PANEL SKIRT

←A→   ←C→

←D→

←B→

Four panel skirt
N.B. A, B, C, D must add up to waist measurement

360° CIRCLE SKIRT— note the more flamboyant look & sweeping movement of the full circle skirt. ➤

WAIST

360° CIRCLE SKIRT
basic circle skirt pattern
cut on the bias

HEM

N.B. fabric is folded over double

GLOVES

gloves

Elbow-length, pink cotton gloves, with a tucked bow.

Short nylon, with loose ruffles.

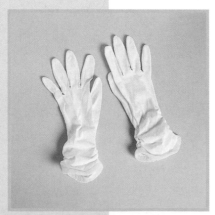

Fine gloves with pleats and gathers.

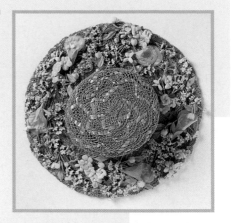

hats

HATS

BAGS

In the past, hats and gloves had associations of formality —weddings and church on Sunday mornings—or privilege —suburban ladies' lunches, Ascot, and garden parties. The workmanship was very fine, and many of the gloves I find are handmade. I don't think of them as something for special occasions, but as an effective throwaway detail.

Handbags are inexpensive and are often made of supple leather, silk-lined, and designed and stitched with a standard of workmanship that would make their price prohibitive today. I often find a purse with an ornate clasp that seems almost royal, or sometimes I find a couture label. One of my favorite flea-market buys is a floral sewing bag with a light wooden handle. I carry it sometimes when I am wearing jeans and a white tee-shirt. It is one of the prettiest accessories I own, and people stop me in the street to admire it. These sewing bags are still easy to come by and not expensive. They were, however, meant to hold sewing—not bunches of keys and a Filofax—and should be treated with the care and respect their age and delicacy deserves.

Well-designed and once-expensive luggage often shows up at flea markets. It lasts forever and is worth considering for good-looking storage or other uses. Although it is often sophisticated and reminiscent of a time when the emphasis was on the voyage rather than the destination, it tends to be too large and heavy for the airline shuttle.

I discovered this ethnic, embroidered, secondhand sack in an old store in England. It comes on many flea-market trips now.

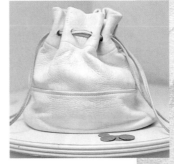

Classic, soft white leather drawstring purse. These bags are at the flea market by the dozen.

A vintage sewing bag gives me much pleasure and will one day be the inspiration for a new Shabby Chic fabric.

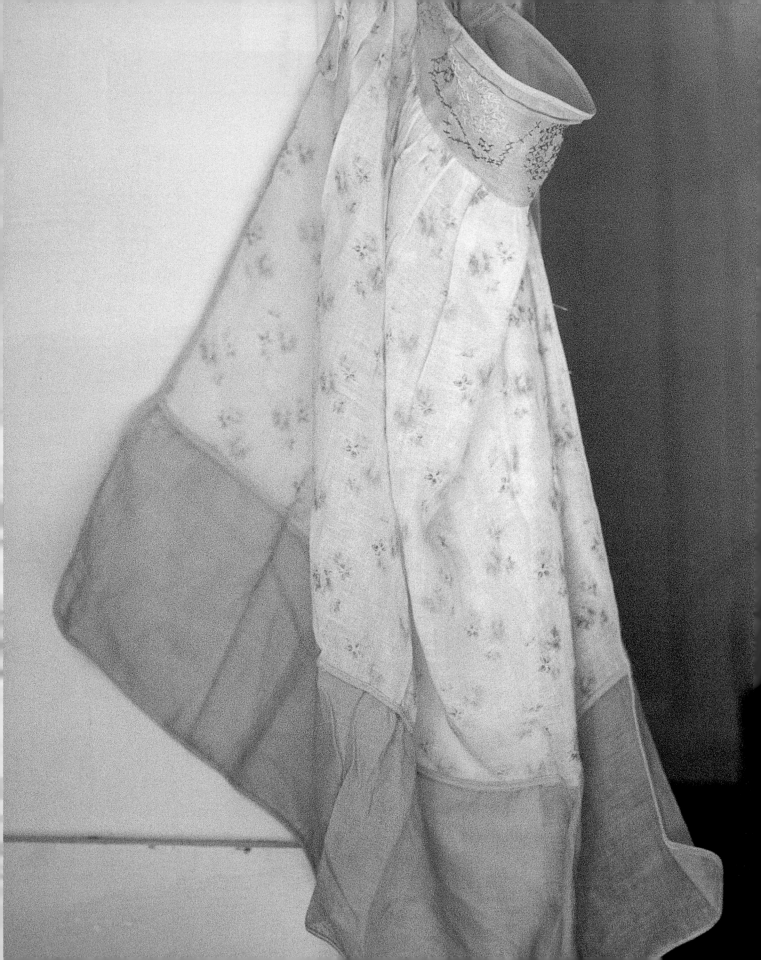

Whatever became of the conversations
that took place after the
"you wash and I'll dry," decision was reached?

chapter 7
FINISHED HOMES 7

FINISHED HOMES
The Full Circle

My home is never quite "finished." It is a living thing and as such develops and changes. My furniture and fabrics become older and worn; they settle in and evolve. New life is introduced by the changes I make, some as permanent as painting a room, some as temporary as buying a bunch of flowers. My house is lived in, for living in. One of the places I find new life is at flea markets.

It may take me a few trips to find what I am looking for. And even when I do, more time may be required to restore it. Instant gratification is not an expectation here, nor would I wish it to be. To get something right, and for it to truly reflect my personality and taste, takes time.

This chapter will look at several homes that are "finished" to the extent that they are comfortably lived in by people of taste and discrimination, "unfinished" in the sense that they are living, changing places.

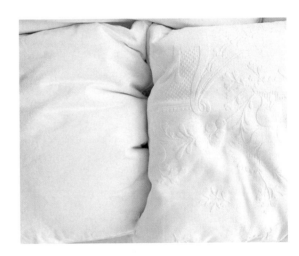

A touch of class is added to a huge, slipcovered Shabby Chic sofa by mixing pieces of a vintage bedcover with basic white denim. I am able to use slightly damaged—and more economical—bedcovers here, because I can cut around any flaws. The sofa wraps around a flea-market coffee table. Once upon a time it was a clunky oak table. I added some simple beaded molding (available at a good hardware store) to give it just a little glamour and then painted it cream. All contribute to a cozy space for Jake.

A fine lawn bedcover doubles as a curtain. In my office at home, I need only to diffuse the light.

MY HOME

My house is lived in, for living in, and for life. Balance is one aspect of this philosophy: a balance of function, beauty, and comfort. My living room contains flowers and a piano for life, good lighting for function, and beautiful, enveloping seating for comfort. The flea-market coffee table was originally a dark clunky oak—I added beading and molding and painted it a calming cream. Instead of heavy and cumbersome, it is now lighter, delicate—in harmony with the room. I made an antique bedcover into large, comfortable, and decorative cushions, which add a touch of class and a cozy invitation to the white denim slipcovers on my Shabby Chic sofa. My office has gradually accumulated a series of objects that are just "off." Each on its own would not quite make it, but in combination they make my surroundings an inspiring and stimulating place to work. Beauty and balance bring peace. So does an acceptance of the impermanence of both living and inanimate objects. The flowers die and are replaced with others equally beautiful but different. A piece of the china we use for dinner breaks. We are sorry to lose it, but because we eat off plates in a harmony of colors and shapes rather than a pattern that matches exactly, the piece will be replaced. The set of china will continue, slightly different, perhaps slightly richer. This re-using of the old, the worn, and the shabby allows objects to meet their natural fate.

An abundance of certain items in the bathroom represents luxury to me, such as white towels and an array of soaps. Here wouldn't be the usual spot for watercolors—but why not? Every area deserves decor. This practical mirror was a flea-market find—the shelf detail makes it for me.

(opposite page)
This is one of my most creative spots in the whole world. A dear friend of mine painted this happy picture for me. The desk was a Carpenteria find, and what was once a patio table I transformed into a seat by adding a cushion.

356

This small pink desk from Summerland Antiques passed my inspection, allowing its somewhat cumbersome wooden knobs to remain. The white wicker bench has an oversized pillow plopped on it.

This tall, slender chest of drawers makes a lovely pedestal for this doll house.

Gathers tacked in place with a tiny bow create a ruffle of perfection. A lampshade poised on a hand-painted glass lamp base is a cozy accessory.

359

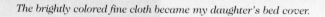

The brightly colored fine cloth became my daughter's bed cover.

A hand-painted trash can—quite a common find —is a nice excuse for more flowers.

This was one of those odd items that caught my eye, because I knew that one day I would find a use for it. Now it is a dumping ground for my daughter's hair accessories.

This pink shelf was hung without further ado. It was the pink that caught my eye.

Sue Balmforth had a local upholsterer restore the original frame of her sofa. She added "tons" of down to bring her cushions back to plump life; she then slipcovered the whole piece in lovely floppy yellow linen. The ottoman, covered loosely in a nineteenth-century toile fabric, is forced to do double duty when a 1940s silver tray is placed on it. (It was found dull at the flea market and polished until it shone).

SUE BALMFORTH AND BOUNTIFUL

The home in which change is most constant and most evident belongs to Sue Balmforth. Sue is a designer who lives on the premises of Bountiful, her antiques shop. The large-scale architectural elements, statuary, and columns make the atmosphere of Bountiful dramatic and theatrical. Sue is dedicated to her work and has a fabulous eye; she keeps an enormous stock so there is a luxurious feeling of plenty—more beautiful French and Italian chandeliers twinkling overhead than you could imagine; lovely, flaky, painted Early American country armoires; European dressers and vanities hand painted in pale colors with floral details and carved rose moldings; quantities of fine wicker chairs hanging from the ceiling. Bountiful is arranged so that there is an opulent sense of layering—vignettes leading to further vignettes, the mercury glass story leading to the crystal story in turn leading to the looking-glass story—and one can see the range of beautiful objects, giving a generous depth of comparison. Sue understood the potential uses of architectural salvage very early on, transforming it into coffee tables, large mirrors, candlesticks, and picture frames.

This is Beatrice, Sue's favorite creature in the whole world.

Sue's scrumptious bedroom can vary from week to week and shipment to shipment. Today it contains a delicate nineteenth-century French antique bedroom suite and is lit by a gorgeous handmade French chandelier, yet can still accept a humble breakfast tray. This 1920s handpainted American tray would have been given as a wedding gift years ago. A thought! Penni Oliver, a friend and associate of Sue at Bountiful, has created a line of lamp shades. She collects pieces of vintage textile and lace, which she then painstakingly hand-sews into delicate one-of-a-kind shades.

A vignette at Bountiful. Once again showing Sue's acceptance of mixing whimsy with the serious. Chipped bowling pins and painted trays from the flea market stand proudly under the twinkle of a posh chandelier.

One of Sue's genius creations is the use of salvaged tin ceilings to frame old paintings found on her travels. A quiet collection of lavender bottles dispels any sense of intimidation. A humble iron outdoor table is as significant as the company it keeps.

Her restoration of damaged pieces is very loyal to the original—broken chandelier drops are replaced with antique crystal; furniture is mended with hardware and hinges from the correct period. Because the objects in her home are part of her stock, they are constantly sold and replaced. The transient nature of her surroundings and possessions might cause anxiety and disorientation in a less adaptable person, but because Sue is original and ingenious, it merely gives scope to her imaginative creativity.

I particularly admire and enjoy Sue's confident mixture of flea-market finds with her up-market antiques. She says, "The accessories are absolutely key to creating a look when you decorate." Everything in Bountiful is for sale—including her bed and the elegant vintage linen that dresses it.

At the edge of Sue Balmforth's bedroom today sits a beautiful, friendly, pale green chair ready to be plopped into place. To me it's like Cinderella waiting to go to the ball. The chair is a 1920s American reproduction of a French chair, so it will easily fit in with her upscale French furniture.

M.L. rescued this decorative floral print from the trash.

M. L. PEACOR

M. L. Peacor is also a designer. Perhaps her greatest design achievement is her own home. She chose her house—a 1930s cottage—for architectural excellence and location rather than size (650 square feet), and her use of space could be a lesson to us all. There is in the entire house no wasted or hidden space; M.L. has made a virtue of storage, and because all containers are in plain view, they clearly reflect her palette—creamy shades of white, yellow, blue, and green. The pale blue drugstore folders for her files, the glazed jars that hold her pencils—all blend with the bare books on her shelves. M.L. dislikes the bright and discordant contrasts of dust jackets and prefers the muted greens, grays, and blues of the books themselves.

In order to accommodate herself and her two sons in an essentially small but aesthetically pleasing space, M.L. has cleverly made most key items of furniture serve more than one function. At night her living room becomes her bedroom: her cushy yellow linen Shabby Chic sleeper sofa becomes her bed, with pastel poplin sheets, down pillows, and a duvet; the pale green painted picnic bench from the dining room becomes her bedside table. Because everything has its place, M.L. can quickly and easily make the space change from one function to another in a way that never compromises.

There are no hidden corners in M.L.'s functional home. Her Shabby Chic sleeper sofa is opened every night as her living room transforms into her bedroom. A pale green painted picnic bench borrowed from the dining room converts into her bedside table at night. In the distance the same pale green paint is used on a basket that holds bills and sits atop a creamy yellow desk. With everything visible, M.L. takes great care to sustain her palette, down to the littlest detail.

M.L. collects books of interest to her but dislikes dust jackets. Their removal often reveals M.L.'s restrained color palette of greens, gray-greens, and blues.

The house is equally cheerful and visually pleasing at all hours of the day or night. She has a great natural sense of color and an original and creative mind but modestly recounts how sometimes her memory inspires her eye: "I just need to see something in an expensive store once and then I know to look out for these things in other places." She describes how she bought a "frog" (the wire bases that stabilize flower arrangements in vases) for her son in an expensive shop—he saw it and really wanted it for "putting little things in"—some time later she saw a similar frog at a rummage sale and picked it up for a dollar. Sometimes we have to see an object in a grander context to recognize its real value.

M.L. got these wonderful, dusty, green, old-fashioned folders from a drugstore. She files and categorizes tear sheets from magazines, which she later refers to when on a design job. She applied flea-market-found jam jar labels for easy identification.

This work table doubles as everything does in M.L.'s compact home. It was originally from Scotland; she painted it pale green and then cleverly added an old wooden tape measure to the side to make measuring fabric easy.

Andrea found this frame dark and containing a portrait from the 1800s. Her beautiful rendering of lilacs now takes its place.

ANDREA AND BRUCE DERN

Andrea Dern is an artist, whose floral oil paintings I love. She and her husband, actor Bruce Dern, live in a house overlooking the ocean in Malibu.

Although the Dern house is quite large—an ever-expanding cottage, enchanted, rambling, full of little staircases and extraordinary light—every room feels as though it is lived in. The Derns have been there for twenty-five years, and Andrea, with a combination of time, life, taste, flowers, and lots of white paint, has produced a home—accented with wicker, flowers, and floral prints—that offers a warm and pleasant atmosphere. The house feels full and at the same time uncluttered. Each object has both its use and its place, and is the result of the imaginative and intelligent blend of materials at hand as well as an artist's taste.

Andrea's studio and her garden overlap. Her flower paintings bring the garden into the studio, and her paintings ensure her house is full of flowers even during the months when her garden is dormant. The briefest visit to Andrea's studio is enough to reveal that she loves what she does, and the environment is one of pleasure in creation, of life enhanced by the smell of the paint mingled with the scent of the flowers. Her artist's eye has designed a garden that is free-form, loose, and inextricably linked to her art. Andrea knows a good deal about her plants and flowers. Not only does she paint them and arrange them in vases around her house but she plants them and takes care of her garden herself.

Andrea and Bruce moved into this wonderful beach cottage twenty-five years ago. Very little in their home has escaped whitewash. The floors and the hutch were all transformed with white paint treatments in varying degrees.

This is Andrea's favorite cup in the world.

(opposite page)
Andrea found this somewhat irregular frame at Bountiful and loved it so much that she painted a picture to fit. The roses are Madam Alfred Carriere (rose paintings available at Shabby Chic).

The Violet Room—this room contains Andrea's gardening books among a theme of violet (her mother's name). The desk came with the house. She painted it white and added a mirror on top for extra reflective light.

Andrea's painting brushes.
Andrea's painting palette.

(previous spread)
Andrea's art studio has a natural
evolution. Although this space
wasn't designed, pieces of furniture
were added as needed. Consequently
it has a strong sense of function
and necessity.

Andrea painted large checks atop this common rush mat, which created a unique effect and made the mat less susceptible to spills and crumbs in the seams. Brilliant!

Andrea applied her talents to this simple round mat, too.

This white vanity from Shabby Chic sits quietly in reflection.

Andrea's style is clever but not contrived; she creates a theme and avoids perfection. There is reasoning to her ways.

This is Andrea and Bruce's other living space. A tall dark dining table became a short white coffee table. Even the standing lamp that was once brass got the white treatment.

Nestled in Andrea's friendly garden, I found baskets in the colors of my palette.

Andrea and Bruce's Badger naps in a bundle of laundry placed in a lovely basket and stand from Bountiful.

A mirror found by Andrea at Shabby Chic was fit for royalty, but had been toned down with a whitewash.

Andrea's garden—her inspiration for her art— her roses, allowed to grow informally, create an air of tolerance.

When Andrea's garden needs a gentle watering, these do the job. The moral of this story is, "Don't walk away from something if the color is wrong."

A mercury glass ball, placed casually on a stick in Andrea and Bruce's garden. A gem.

Tucked away among the flowers, this happy girl poses. Little chips here and there are acceptable, as with all of us.

*The shell mirror was the first purchase Andrea made
when she and Bruce moved into their home. Inexpensive,
it creates an eclectic corner in which to reflect.*

This small dining room of Andrea and Bruce's was cleverly expanded with the simple use of mirrors (beveled, of course). Once again tables and chairs are white. Andrea wonders whether it's time to give the table a new coat —I advise her not to, because I believe it's at the perfect stage of chic now.

A collection of Depression glass sparkles, as fine as any crystal.

Barry and Lili Gross uncovered this stunning stenciling that frames their entranceway while they were renovating their house. Such detail deserves to be complemented. A French chandelier welcomes their guests. The friendly, unassuming hand-hooked rug balances the informal elegance. A flea-market dresser is adorned with a selection of shells and dried flower displays.

BARRY AND LILI GROSS

Barry and Lili Gross live in a 1940s Spanish-style house on the beach that exudes hospitality, comfort, and warmth. These qualities—and a mixture of tradition and elegant bohemianism—become evident as soon as one comes through the door. The stenciling around the entranceway was uncovered when they renovated the house—a pleasant surprise under layers of wallpaper—and the cement is chipped and flaked so the pattern is mottled and irregular. Usually I find stenciling a little too perfect, but here the uneven surface causes it to take on some of the qualities of a trompe l'oeil. The Grosses celebrated this find by dressing up the space with a French chandelier—mostly crystal but with a sprinkling of purple drops—and, for balance and contrast, a welcoming and humble hooked rug.

The house's essential feeling is one of family and fiesta. There is constant relaxed entertaining and someone always seems to be napping. The design and decor of the beach house is geared toward the comfort and feeding—with delicacies always arranged in an appetizing and original way—of a large number of family and friends. In the living room a large stack of futons is covered by an even larger white denim sack—an original, almost eccentric choice in an otherwise traditional room. Covered with cushions, like every other comfortable surface in the house or on the deck, it invites you to plop down wherever you are. The practical white denim can be unzipped and laundered when there is a build-up of sea salt or if a guest spills a glass of wine.

(opposite page) Barry and Lili's princess. Her room is decorated with flea-market finds and vintage textiles. Susie Cohen (Lili's sister), a designer, combined scraps of vintage lace, damask, and floral broadcloth to create a dreamlike window treatment for her niece's bedroom. The velvet throne is paired with a modest needlepoint footstool. The headboard and bedside table are fun, inexpensive, found treasures, able to withstand inevitable sticky hands and doodles.

On Barry and Lili's shaded deck sits a royal blue tiled table, which got the white treatment for its legs, giving it a French Provincial feel. Their plastic patio furniture is made stylish by covering the seat cushions with unexpectedly classy fabric and then layering them with old pieces of beaded cloth.

A carefully and hospitably planned deck has a balance of sun and shade; the furniture is practical and comfortable—huge futons in spring floral colors, covers made by a local seamstress, and extravagantly fine fabric on the cushions lend a touch of grandeur to the functional plastic outdoor furniture. There is a cheerful jumble of color, and the essential ordinariness of basic outdoor furniture is transformed by Barry and Lili's concentration on pleasure and function. There is an inviting hammock, and quantities of beach towels are stacked in a large wooden poled box.

Five houses. The sizes and functions vary from an elegant antiques shop, whose owner lives on the premises, to an informal beach house full of guests, children, and dogs to a family who insist on gracious living in the smallest possible space. Yet each home has several things in common. None has been "done" by an outside decorator; none shows evidence of money unnecessarily spent nor of conspicuous consumption; each has included worn relics of the past, bought at flea markets, in either their original form or imaginatively adapted for another use. In all these homes the passing of time has seasoned the look and atmosphere. These homes have evolved not by being left to their own devices but by a watchful, practical, and imaginative eye constantly ensuring that they adapt and grow to serve their function and please the eye while doing so. Balance. Beauty. Comfort.

Barry and Lili's luxurious deck is inexpensively decorated but lacks nothing in comfort and pleasure to the eye. Basic futons are hidden with easily removable floral chintz covers (made by a local seamstress). Mix-and-match collections of throw pillows are tossed around casually. Bath mats act as rugs. A wooden poled box is home to an assortment of towels.

Friendly birds sit on Andrea's table.

BLESS THIS HOUSE

BLESS this house, O Lord we pray,
    Make it safe by night and day;
Bless these walls, so firm and stout,
    Keeping want and trouble out;
Bless the roof and chimney tall;
    Let Thy peace lie over all;
Bless this door, that it may be
    Ever wide to welcome Thee.

a prayer for my home.

Sav-on

70% Isopropyl
Rubbing
Alcohol

Rubefaciente

16 FL OZ (1 PT) 473 mL

WD-40

®

• Stops Squeaks
• Protects Metal
• Loosens Rusted Parts
• Frees Sticky Mechanisms

Rit
LIQUID DYE

UNSCENTED EXTRA SUPER HOLD

QUA
ET

ssional
Hair Spray

The
Original

Woolite
FINE FABRIC WASH

CARE YOU CAN TRUST
No Shrinking, Stretching, Fading

354925   16 FL OZ (1 PT)

BROWN

RESOURCES

8

chapter 8

FABRIC CARE

Washing

'WOOLITE' IS RECOMMENDED FOR WASHING ANY DELICATE FABRICS, VINTAGE CLOTHING, LINGERIE, SILKS, AND WOOL BLANKETS. USE COLD WATER, SOAK AND RINSE WELL. AIR DRY. OLD WOOLEN BLANKETS MAY BE MACHINE WASHED WITH WOOL-ITE TO SOFTEN THEM. AIR DRY, PREFERABLY OUTSIDE.

WASHING LACE: ANYTHING WITH LACE EDGING SHOULD BE HAND-WASHED. LAY FLAT TO DRY AND WHILE STILL DAMP, PAT INTO SHAPE WITH YOUR FINGERS. IT IS A GOOD IDEA TO WAIT FOR LACE TO DRY COMPLETELY BEFORE ATTEMPTING TO IRON IT.

CLEANING VINTAGE LINENS: WASH IN WARM WATER WITH A MILD DETERGENT AND A NON-CHLORINE BLEACH LIKE 'CLOROX 2' ON THE GENTLE CYCLE. FOLLOW BLEACHING DIRECTIONS ON THE PACKAGE. DELICATE PIECES SHOULD BE WASHED BY HAND. FOR STUBBORN STAINS, TRY A CHLORINE BLEACH SUCH AS REGULAR 'CLOROX' OR 'SNOWY BLEACH', BUT BEAR IN MIND, SOME OLDER OR FRAGILE PIECES MAY NOT STAND THE STRAIN OF BLEACHING OR EVEN MACHINE WASHING. FOR A NATURAL BLEACHING AGENT TRY RUBBING A STAIN WITH A LEMON CUT IN HALF. *

Bleaching

NEVER POUR BLEACH DIRECTLY ONTO FABRIC. ALWAYS DILUTE BLEACH BEFORE ADDING FABRICS TO THE WATER. IT IS A GOOD IDEA TO TEST THE FABRIC FIRST BEFORE BLEACHING THE ENTIRE PIECE. SOME FABRICS MAY YELLOW FROM BLEACHING AND SOME OLDER FABRICS MAY FALL APART. THERE IS ALWAYS A BIT OF RISK WITH THIS METHOD.

THE 'CLOROX' CO. DOES NOT RECOMMEND USING BLEACH FOR FADING AS IT CAN RESULT IN AN UNEVEN LOOK AKIN TO TIE-DYE. TO REMOVE COLOR THEY RECOMMEND 'RIT' OR 'TINTEX' COLOR REMOVER. FOR QUESTIONS ABOUT USING BLEACH, YOU CAN CALL THE 'CLOROX' CO. AT: (800) 292 2808 FROM 9 AM → 5.30 PM E.S.T.

Tea Staining

(NOTE: THE FOLLOWING TECHNIQUE RESULTS IN AN ATTRACTIVE, BUT NOT PERMANENT EFFECT.)

TO AGE FABRICS WITH A GENTLE OVERALL CREAM COLOR, SOAK IN A BATH OF TEA WATER. MAKE A TEABAG SOLUTION WITH WARM WATER. AFTER SOAKING THE ARTICLE RINSE WELL IN COLD WATER. THE NUMBER OF TEABAGS TO AMOUNT OF WATER AND LENGTH OF SOAK TIME DEPENDS ON QUANTITY OF FABRIC, HOW FAST A PARTICULAR FABRIC TAKES THE COLOR AND THE DARKNESS DESIRED.(THE COLOR WILL BE LIGHTER WHEN DRY, AND NATURAL FABRICS TAKE COLOR MORE READILY THAN SYNTHETIC ONES.) THIS IS A TECHNIQUE THAT REQUIRES YOU TO EXPERIMENT!

Dying

'RIT' DYE IS EASY TO COME BY AND IS EVEN SOLD AT MANY SUPERMARKETS. IT COMES IN A POWDERED OR LIQUID FORM. THE LIQUID IS EASIER TO USE TO OBTAIN AN EVEN RESULT. FOR DYING FABRICS, FOLLOW DIRECTIONS ON PACKAGE.

Color Removal

Rit COLOR REMOVER

TO FADE OUT FABRICS WHICH MAY BE TOO BRIGHTLY COLORED USE A COLOR REMOVER PRODUCT SUCH AS ONES MANUFACTURED BY 'RIT' OR 'TINTEX'.

* AN OLD TIME WAY OF REMOVING STAINS FROM TABLE LINENS IS TO LAY THEM OUTSIDE ON THE GRASS BEFORE SUNDOWN AND LET THE DEW SOAK IN OVERNIGHT. IT IS SAID THE DEW WILL DRAW OUT THE STAINS AND THE SUN WILL FINISH BLEACHING THEM CLEAN THE NEXT DAY.

N.B. WHEN WORKING WITH THE ABOVE METHODS (E.G. DYING, STAINING, BLEACHING ETC.) IT IS ADVISABLE TO WEAR RUBBER GLOVES.

TIPS FOR TRANSFORMING TREASURES

USE ALCOHOL TO REMOVE GLUE RESIDUE FROM GLOSSY PORCELAIN. GLUE SHOULD BE GENTLY ABRADED WITH AN EMERY BOARD FIRST, AND THEN WIPED WITH A SOFT CLOTH DIPPED IN RUBBING ALCOHOL. TO CLEAN THE CRYSTALS ON CHANDELIERS, WIPE WITH A CLOTH MOISTENED WITH ALCOHOL.

A SINK FULL OF WARM WATER, NOT HOT, MIXED WITH 1/4 CUP OF CLEAR AMMONIA IS EXCELLENT FOR CLEANING GLASS. SOAK FOR A FEW MINUTES, THEN RINSE AND DRY GENTLY. NEVER PUT OLD GLASS PIECES IN THE DISHWASHER. SEE: MISCELLANEOUS SIDEBAR.

SOME SMALL PAINTBRUSHES ARE USEFUL FOR GENTLE CLEANING OF INTRICATE PORCELAIN FIGURES, VASES, LAMPS AND SUCH. YOU CAN EASILY DUST AND REMOVE GRIME FROM CREVICES AND DECORATIVE MOLDINGS WITH A CLEAN, SOFT BRISTLE BRUSH. KEEP SOME ON HAND FOR SMALL PAINT REPAIR JOBS ON VASES OR LAMPS.

CLEAN STAINED ENAMELWARE BY SOAKING FOR AN HOUR OR TWO IN A BATH OF ONE TABLESPOON OF BAKING SODA ADDED TO A SINKFUL OF HOT SOAPY WATER. TO REMOVE PENCIL, INK OR CRAYON MARKS FROM WALLS OR PAINTED SURFACES, RUB WITH A DAMP CLOTH DIPPED IN DRY BAKING SODA. THIS CAN BE USED TO RUB OFF COFFEE OR TEA STAINS ON CHINA CUPS.

TO CLEAN POLISHED MARBLE, USE WHITE CHALK MOISTENED WITH A LITTLE BIT OF WATER AND RUB GENTLY.

USE TO BRIGHTEN WHITE LINENS AND VINTAGE FABRICS. SEE: FABRIC CARE SECTION

REINFORCE JOINTS ON WOODEN CHAIRS AND TABLES, AND MAKE SMALL REPAIRS TO PICTURE FRAMES OR SHELVES WITH THIS GLUE. FOR A GOOD BOND, APPLY TO BOTH SIDES AND SECURE WHILE DRYING WITH SOME SORT OF CLAMPING DEVICE OR STRING UNTIL THE FOLLOWING DAY.

GESSO CAN EASILY BE USED FOR A WHITE-WASH FINISH ON WOODEN FURNITURE. USED BY ARTISTS FOR PREPARING CANVAS, IT CAN BE FOUND IN ART SUPPLY STORES.

HAIRSPRAY CAN BE USED TO REMOVE MARKING PEN, TAPE AND PRICE STICKER RESIDUE FROM GLASS. SPRAY ON AND WIPE OFF THOROUGHLY. SPRAY HAIRSPRAY ON ROSES TO PRESERVE THEM AND HANG THE FLOWERS UPSIDE DOWN UNTIL THEY HAVE DRIED COMPLETELY, AT LEAST ONE WEEK.

A LEMON, CUT IN HALF AND DIPPED IN SALT, CAN BE USED TO REMOVE TARNISH FROM OLD COPPER ITEMS. LEMON CAN BE RUBBED ONTO FABRIC STAINS SUCH AS INK, JUICE, OR RUST AS A NATURAL STAIN REMOVER.

AIRPLANE MODEL PAINT CAN BE PURCHASED AT ANY HOBBY STORE AND MANY TOY STORES. IT IS GOOD TO KEEP A SUPPLY OF COLORS ON HAND TO MAKE TOUCH-UP REPAIRS ON LAMPS, CERAMIC, PORCELAIN, FURNITURE, ETC.

A GREAT TOUCH-UP PRODUCT FOR CHIPS ON VASES AND OTHER PAINTED SURFACES. IT IS WATERPROOF WHEN DRY, AND COMES IN A MYRIAD OF PASTELS AND BRIGHTS SO YOU CAN EASILY MATCH COLORS.

THIS IS A VERY EASY WAY TO REMOVE OLD TAPE AND PRICE TAG RESIDUE. JUST RUB A VERY SMALL AMOUNT OF PEANUT BUTTER ON THE STICKY TAG WITH YOUR FINGER AND WIPE OR WASH OFF. WORKS WELL ON GLASS, COPPER AND BRASS.

'RIT' DYE IS SOLD IN POWDERED OR LIQUID FORM IN ABOUT 50 COLORS. IT IS EASIER TO OBTAIN AN EVEN HUE WITH THE LIQUID AS YOU DON'T HAVE TO WORRY ABOUT THE DYE CRYSTALS DISSOLVING COMPLETELY. SEE: FABRIC CARE SECTION. IT CAN ALSO BE USED TO STAIN UNFINISHED WOOD FURNITURE, FRAMES OR SMALL SHELVES IN A VARIETY OF SHADES. SEE: MISCELLANEOUS SIDEBAR.

KEEP SOME SANDPAPER ON HAND FOR QUICK REPAIRS TO ROUGH EDGES. THE FINEST SAND- PAPERS GIVE THE GENTLEST EFFECT. EVEN EMERY BOARDS ARE HANDY FOR GETTING INTO SMALL PLACES.

YOU CAN USE A BLACK OR BROWN SHOE POLISH TO DARKEN OVER-BRIGHT METAL HINGES ON CABINETS. APPLY SPARINGLY WITH A SOFT CLOTH AND RUB INTO GROOVES. THIS IS NOT PERMANENT AND ALSO SHOULD NOT BE USED NEAR FABRIC OR ON PLACES WHERE PEOPLE WILL TOUCH, SUCH AS DRAWER PULLS OR KNOBS.

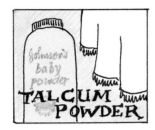

TALCUM POWDER IS A GOOD AID IN STAIN REMOVAL. REMOVE AS MUCH OF THE STAIN AS POSSIBLE BY BLOTTING WITH A CLEAN CLOTH. APPLY TALCUM POWDER AND LET IT SIT UNTIL THE POWDER BECOMES DISCOLORED BY ABSORBING THE STAIN; ABOUT 10 MINUTES. WIPE OFF WITH A CLEAN CLOTH. REPEAT IF NECESSARY.

IMMERSING FABRICS IN A BATH OF TEABAGS AND WARM WATER WILL IMPART A DELICATE AGED TONE TO THE CLOTH. SEE: FABRIC CARE SECTION.

VERY FINE GRADE STEEL WOOL DIPPED IN REGULAR VEGETABLE OIL CAN BE USED TO GENTLY RUB OFF THE RUST ADHERING TO OLD CUTLERY AND METAL HARDWARE.

WASH OLD BLANKETS IN 'WOOLITE' TO SOFTEN THEM. SEE: FABRIC CARE SECTION.

INDEX OF INTERIOR DESIGNERS

AND DESIGN SERVICES REFERRED TO IN THIS BOOK

Sue Balmforth
Bountiful
1335 Abbot Kinney Road
Venice, CA 90291
(310) 450-3620

Karin Blake
Karin Blake Interiors
49 A Malibu Colony
Malibu, CA 90265
(310) 456-8010

Susan Cohen
Susan Cohen Interiors
2118 Wilshire Boulevard, Suite 962
Santa Monica, CA 90403
(310) 828-4445

M. L. Peacor
M. L. Peacor Interior Design
1126 Idaho Avenue
Santa Monica, CA 90403
(310) 451-7787

Shabby Chic – Los Angeles
1013 Montana Avenue
Santa Monica, CA 90403
(310) 394-1975

Shabby Chic – Chicago
54 East Walton Street
Chicago, IL 60611
(312) 649-0080

Bryan Wark
2nd Street Holdings, Inc.
628 San Quan Avenue
Venice, CA 90291
(310) 396-9072

*The entrance to the opulent world of Bountiful,
the home of Sue Balmforth.*

PERIODICALS:

Antique Journal
1684 Decoto Road, Suite 166
Union City, CA 95487
(800) 791-8592; (510) 791-8592

Northern California, Oregon, and Nevada
Monthly newspaper, available free at 1,500
California locations, stores, auctions, and bookstores.

Antiques and Collectibles
500 Fesler Street, Suite 201
El Cajon, CA 92020
(619) 593-2925

Southern California, Arizona, and Nevada
Monthly newspaper, available free at antiques malls
and stores.

Antique Trader
P.O. Box 1050
Dubuque, IA 52004
(800) 334-7165

Weekly national publication, sold by subscription.
Classified, calendar of shows, markets, and
auctions listed by state.

Clark's Flea Market USA
5469 Inland Cove Court
Milton, FL 32583
(850) 623-0794

National directory of events, sold by
subscription, published four times a year.

Maine Antique Digest
P.O. Box 1429
911 Main Street
Waldoboro, ME 04572
(800) 752-8521

East Coast monthly periodical, sold by subscription.
Classified, calendar of shows by advertisers.
U.S. and international listings.

Cotton & Quail Antique Trail
P.O. Box 326
Monticello, FL 32345
(800) 757-7755; (850) 997-3880

Covers the nine Southern states: Kentucky, Tennessee,
North Carolina, South Carolina, Alabama, Georgia,
Florida, Mississippi, and Louisiana. Monthly antique
periodical with four-month auction and show calendar.

Warman's Today's Collector
700 East State Street
Iola, WI 54990-0001
(800) 258-0929

National monthly publication, for sale at newsstands.
Articles, events listed by state, and classified section.

BOOKS

Antique Atlas
By Ken Leggett
Rainy Day Publishing Co.
Sourcebook with state-by-state listing of
antiques shops across the United States.

The Official Directory to U.S. Flea Markets
Edited by Kitty Werner
House of Collectibles

Price Guide to Flea Market Treasures
By Harry L. Rinker Jr.
Krause Publishing
List of choice U.S. flea markets and publications.

U.S. Flea Market Directory
By Albert La Farge
Avon Books

Maloney's Antiques and Collection Resource Directory
By David Maloney
Antique Trader Books

MASSACHUSETTS
BRIMFIELD:
Crystal Brook Antique Show (413) 245-7647

J & J Promotions Antiques & Collectibles Shows (413) 245-3436

New England Motel Antiques Market (508) 347-2179

Shelton Antique Shows (413) 245-3591

Route 20, near Sturbridge

Hours: Held three times a year (usually beginning the second Tuesday of May, the Tuesday after the Fourth of July, and the Tuesday after Labor Day in September). Market runs from dawn on Tuesday through 5:00 p.m. Sunday. Call for exact dates.
Admission: Varies from free to $5.00. Parking is usually around $5.00.

The Brimfield market is actually a series of about 22 markets that run more or less consecutively over five days in May, July, and September. It is virtually a whole town full of antiques and collectibles with some 400 vendors spread over many acres of land. It is often referred to as the best market in the country.

MICHIGAN
ANN ARBOR:
Ann Arbor Antiques Market

5055 Ann Arbor Saline Road. Exit 175 off I-94, go south three miles
Ann Arbor, MI 48103
(313) 662-9453

Hours: Third Sunday of the month, April–November. 6:00 a.m. to 4:00 p.m.
Extra shows in April and November. Admission: $5.00 per person. Free parking.

30 years in operation, 350 dealers of good-quality antiques. All dealers screened and referenced.

NEW MEXICO
SANTA FE:
Trader Jack's Flea Market

Seven miles north of Santa Fe on Highway 285 (505) 455-7874

Hours: Every Friday, Saturday, and Sunday, 7:00 a.m. to 6:00 p.m. Free parking.

This flea market operates about nine months a year, weather permitting. Open since 1975.

SOUTH CAROLINA
CHARLESTON:
Low County Flea Market & Collectibles

77 Calhoun Street at the Gaillard Auditorium
(803) 884-7204 / 577-7400

Hours: Third weekend of every month and one extra in late November.
Saturdays, 9:00 a.m. to 6:00 p.m. Sundays, 10:00 a.m. to 5:00 p.m. Admission: $2.00 per person

Mostly antiques, collectibles, and estate merchandise.

TENNESSEE

NASHVILLE:

Tennessee State Fairgrounds Flea Market

At the Tennessee State Fairgrounds, at Wedgewood   (615) 862-5016

Hours: Fourth weekend of every month, except in December, when it is held on the third weekend. Saturdays, 6:00 a.m. to 6: 00 p.m. Sundays, 7:00 a.m. to 4:00 p.m. Admission: $2.00 per person

Mostly antiques, collectibles, and estate merchandise.

INTERNATIONAL

For the international listings it is always a good idea to check the dates and times. Mornings are generally a better bet, because things can wind down early. Many cities have weekly or monthly markets. Ask at your hotel for information about local events.

LONDON:

Bermondsey Market (or New Caledonia Market)

South of Tower Bridge / Bermondsey Street and Long Lane. • Hours: 4:00 a.m. to afternoon.

Brick Lane Market

Shoreditch tube station, in East End. • Hours: Sundays, 9:00 a.m.to 2:00 p.m.

Camden Lock Market

Camden Town tube station, Northern Line. • Hours: Sundays, 9:00 a.m. to 5:00 p.m.

Camden Passage Market (Camden Walk Market)

Angel tube station, turn right, then right again. • Hours: Saturdays and Wednesdays, 8:00 a.m. to 4:00 p.m.

Petticoat Lane

Middlesex Street in East End, Liverpool Street, Aldgate, or Aldgate East stop. Hours: Sundays, early to noon (best time).

Portobello Road

West end of London, Notting Hill Gate tube stop. Hours: Saturdays, 5:30 a.m. to 3:00 p.m. for the outdoor market; shops open daily.

PARIS:

Porte de Cligancourt/Marche aux Puces

Metro Station: Porte de Cligancourt Hours: Saturday–Monday, 9:30 a.m. to 6:00 p.m.

The largest flea market in Europe, with more than 1,600 sellers. This location also has a number of satellite markets along its edges comprising several miles of great shopping.

Ocean Beach Antique Mall
4878 Newport Avenue
San Diego, CA 92107
(619) 223-6170

Two stories tall with up to 40 dealers, this mall features traditional American and distressed furniture, accessories, pottery, old hardware, and dollhouses.

Somewhere In Time Antiques
1312 19th Street
Bakersfield, CA 93301
(805) 326-8562

Store with a little bit of everything: pottery, glassware, pitchers, clothing, furniture, etc.

State Street Antique Mall
710 State Street
Santa Barbara, CA 93101
(805) 967-2575

More than 50 dealers with a wide a variety of goods: furniture, vintage linens and clothes, fabrics, antique phones, paintings, and household accessories.

Summerland Hillside Antiques
P.O. Box 1434
Summerland, CA 93067
(805) 565-5226
(805) 565-5226

Antiques, interiors, and treasures. This store features mirrors, lamps, and furniture, from cottage-style to formal.

Tiffany's Antiques
3010 North Center Street
Soquel, CA 95073
(408) 477-9808

Collective with 13 dealers showing a varied selection of cottage- and garden-style, vintage florals, ironwork, pine, oak, and wicker, painted pieces, and lampshades.

Tutti-Fruitti
Diana Weihs
(213) 733-3123

Vintage clothing from the 1930s to 1950s, sold at antiques shows throughout the Los Angeles area.

Vignettes
4828 Newport Avenue
San Diego, CA 92107
(619) 222-9244

Displays set up like rooms and gardens, selling vintage linens and clothing, jewelry, unusual architectural items, ironworks, and furniture from the 1850s to the 1950s.

ARIZONA

The Brass Armadillo
12419 North 28th Drive
I-17 north of Cactus
Phoenix, AZ 85029
(888) 942-0030

610 dealers in 40,000 square-feet. Furniture, architectural items, lighting, and 612 glass-enclosed cases with hundreds of treasures.

CONNECTICUT

Wright's Barn
Wright Road off Route 4
Torrington, CT 06790
(203) 482-0095

An indoor market in a 10,000-square-foot barn with 40 permanent dealers.

IOWA

The Brass Armadillo
701 N.E. 50th Avenue
Des Moines, IA 50313
(515) 262-0092

Large antiques mall housing 400 dealers in 36,000 square feet. Glass, pottery, furniture, and much more.

MICHIGAN

Great Midwestern Antique Emporium
5233 Dixie Highway
Waterford, MI 48329
(248) 623-7460

5,000-square-foot co-op mall housing 50 dealers. Antiques and collectibles—depression glass, pottery, and furniture, from the 1850s to the 1950s.

Kalik's Antiques
198 West Liberty
Plymouth, MI 48329
(313) 455-5595

Eight dealers in the Old Village part of Plymouth featuring military, western, sports, hunting, and fishing antiques; furniture; and collectibles.

NEBRASKA

The Brass Armadillo
10666 Sapp Brothers Drive
Omaha, NE 68138
(800) 896-9140

Another large mall from Brass Armadillo. 350 dealers in 30,000 square feet of space, which features their furniture and selection of books.

NEW MEXICO

El Colectivo
De Vargas Mall / corner of
Passe de Peralta and North Guadeloupe
Santa Fe, NM 87501
(505) 820-7205

Antiques mall with 16 permanent dealers and additional merchandise on consignment. Antiques, collectibles, and out-of-print books.

Majestic Lion Antique Center
5048 2nd Avenue
Des Moines, IA 50313
(515) 282-5466

High-end antiques in a 250-dealer mall. They offer American furniture, accessories, porcelain, pottery, glass, and the entire 35,000-square-foot ceiling full of lighting fixtures.

NEW YORK

Olde Good Things
124 West 24th Street
New York, NY 10011-1904
(212) 989-8401

Solomon's Mine
95 Main Street
Cold Springs, NY 10516
(914) 265-5042

ENGLAND

The Old Haberdasher
141 Portobello Road
Nottinghill Gate
London W11
0181-907-8684

Architectural artifacts salvaged from old New York buildings.
Huge inventory of doorknobs, doors, mantels, hardware,
sinks, tubs, gates, stonework, fences, columns, and a lot more.

Unusual antiques and collectibles. Old medical equipment
and furniture, cameras, mechanical and optical items.

Antique lace, braids, ribbons, trims, and haberdashery.

*The evidence of this hard work makes me think twice
about whether it's fair to bargain too hard.*

*Mission accomplished. Cathy, Pete, and I have just completed
an early morning flea-market buying trip.*

The Divine Ladder

Unto each mortal who comes to earth
A ladder is given by God at birth
And up this ladder every soul must go,
Step by step from the Valley below;
Step by step to the Center of space,
On this ladder of lives, to the Starting place.

In time departed (which yet endures)
I shape my ladder, and you shape yours,
Whatever they are --- they are what we made
A ladder of light, or a ladder of shade,
A ladder of love, or a hateful thing,
A ladder of strength, or a wavering string,
A ladder of gold, or a ladder of straw,
Each is a ladder of a righteous Law.
We flung them away at the Call of Death,
We took them again with the next life breath,
For a Keeper stands at the great birth gates;
As each soul passes, its ladder waits.

Tho mine be narrow, and yours be broad,
On my ladder alone can I climb to God.
On your ladder alone can your feet ascend,
For none may borrow and none may lend.
If toil and trouble and pain are found,
Twisted and corded to form each round,
If rusting iron or mouldering wood
Is the fragile frame, you must make it good;
You must build it over and fashion it strong,
Tho the task be as hard as your life is long;
For up this ladder the pathway leads
To earthly pleasures and spirit needs;
And all that may come in another way
Shall be but illusion and will not stay

In useless effort, then waste no time;
Rebuild your ladder, and Climb and Climb

The end.

NOTES

NOTES

the
SHABBY
CHIC
home

Contents

The most beautiful things in the world cannot be seen

or even touched—they must by felt with the heart.

—HELEN KELLER

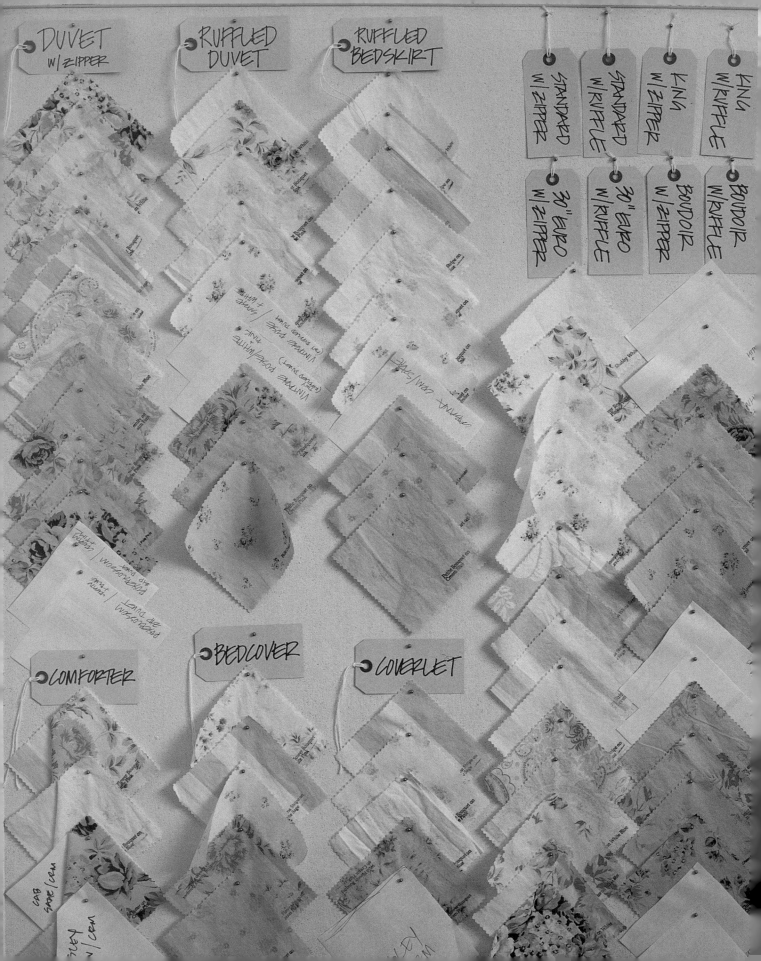

M 61 - Blush w/ Worn White

M 51 - Pale Green w/ White Accent

I asked my broker to arrange another visit. This time I walked in and instantly saw what had to be done. I could see the house's bones—its wonderful wide-plank floors, its old paned sash windows (a rarity in Southern California)—and I fell in love with them, and with the house.

Buying the house was a protracted transaction—no one's fault—and it took nearly a year before I owned it. It was as though I were being tested over and over again as to whether I really did want the house. At times this caused me to think hard, but never to worry.

In renovating the house, budget was again a consideration, so I walked through my new house with my contractor and made two lists: the first, which would account for three quarters of my budget, included the essentials; the second, a wish list of alterations and changes to be done as I could afford them.

It was just a question of getting the house back to its bones. It had been built by a Swedish boatbuilder at the end of the 1920s. His maritime background can be seen in the magnificent floors—very wide and irregular planks—and the basic but securely latched storage areas. A *Hansel and Gretel* theme had been added by a subsequent owner, presumably in the 1940s, and some slicked-up kitchen and bathroom details reflected the taste of later owners. I wanted to take the house back to its origins and then add my own decor.

The essentials all worked toward the same idea: to give the house and grounds light and life. The greater part of the house and guest house were to be painted white, the trees were to be thinned to let in the sun and the sky, the dark pool was to become a turquoise one, and everything that was sad, depressing, gloomy, or downright squalid was to be removed.

Opposite: The heart of a ranunculus.

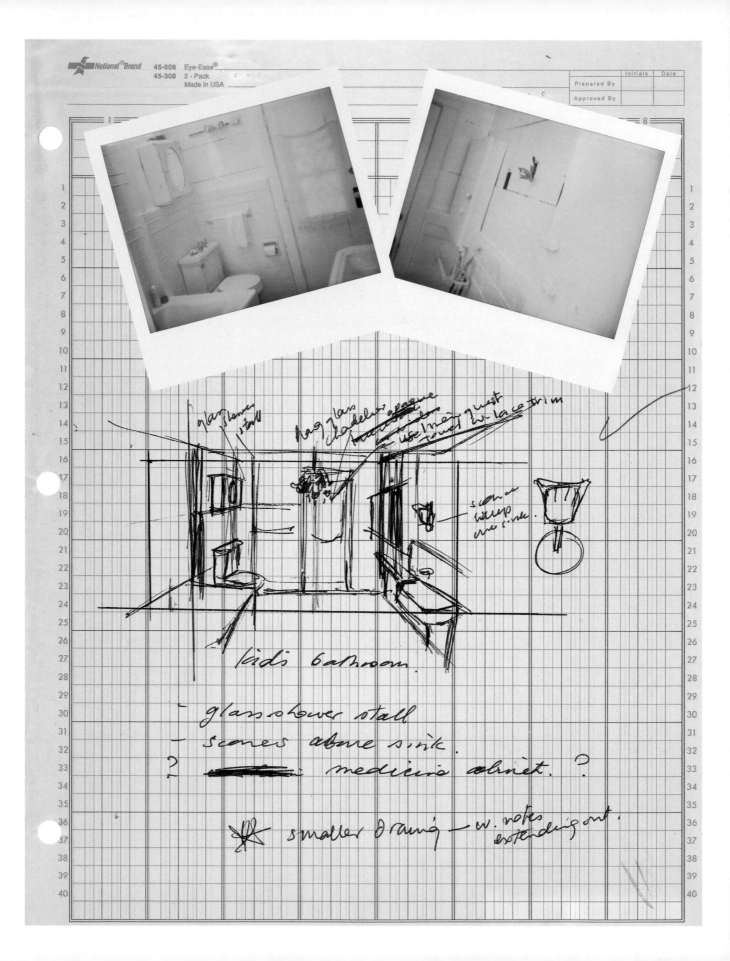

kids bathroom.

- glass shower stall
- sconces above sink.
? ~~————~~ medicine cabinet. ?

✷ smaller drawing — w. notes extending out.

My contractor was surprised that I didn't want to take the opportunity to make larger bathrooms by ripping down walls. But I don't believe in the casual gutting of a newly acquired house. At times my decisions were budget-driven, but even if I could have afforded it I wouldn't have indulged in change merely for change's sake. Rather than gutting a house, I think it makes more sense to keep looking until you find a house whose bones you love and respect, then remove what doesn't work and build on the bones. I leave myself open to the influence of the house itself, rather than imposing my own preexisting ideas on it.

This book is an account of acquiring a house, decorating it, making it a home, and living in it. It describes how I find fixtures and furniture, and look for treasure; how I allow the house itself to give me ideas, to feed my inspiration; how a garden expands my range of color and shape; how I entertain my friends; and how my children and I live in it. This book is an exploration of the expansion of my taste, the progression of my aesthetic ideal and ideas. It explains how I decide what to leave alone, and how I live with small imperfections, and even, sometimes, make a virtue of them.

> *My home—
> someplace I always return to
> that feels just right.*

1

BEFORE
& AFTER

Previous page: The once-creepy tunnel is now a breezy walkway. Not a day goes by that I don't enjoy walking through it from the street. It is like a magical land for me.

AFTER

The Garden & Outdoors

When I bought my house it was a landmark in the neighborhood: the dark wood and huge craggly shutters, painted turquoise, suggested the witch's house in *Hansel and Gretel*. To add to its sinister, mysterious quality, what appeared from the street to be the front door really led into a long, dark passage under the guest house that ended in a dim and overgrown garden. The garden and the out-of-control creeping ivy were home to a large and healthy population of rodents.

Even so, I had bought the house with plans to renovate, not to remodel entirely. I had chosen a house with an infrastructure that did not require rebuilding: It had a sound roof, and the plumbing and electrical wiring were in good condition. With children to raise, a business to run, and a life to lead, I simply don't have the time and money to do work that's not completely necessary. And, anyway, it is more in my nature to ask "Can we keep it?" than to say "Let's tear it out." What I got rid of had to go; I dispose of nothing lightly.

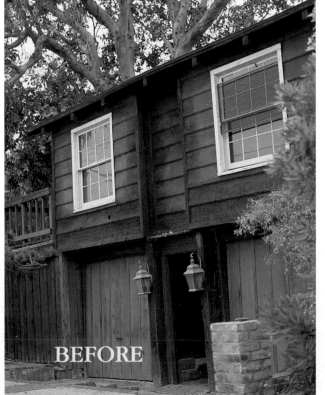

BEFORE

Left: The exterior of the house. Before, it was dark and a little spooky. The turquoise trim didn't help, but coats and coats of white paint did. Indoors, I don't like two tones of color, but on the exterior of my house I like this semi-gloss on the façade and the detail of gloss on the trim.

443

Painting, renovating the pool, thinning the eucalyptus trees, and clearing the jungle aspect of the garden were all part of my list of essentials. All three—representing three quarters of my renovation budget—were aimed at making the house and the garden lighter.

My budget allowed me to spend between 10 and 15 percent of the house's purchase price on renovation. This comparatively modest percentage was adequate, in part because I did not have to tear up anything to rewire or to replace pipes. I could avoid structural alterations, and hence dealing with too much of the unknown, which is where costs tend to get out of hand.

Right: The outside hallway and backyard before renovation—dark and witchy.

Opposite: The witch's haven has been replaced with a heavenly view. I shake out my sheets and look at the lovely setting below—a sun umbrella and teak chaises on the grass and stone. I tried to put down a lawn, but it was impossible because of the shade of the eucalyptus and the chlorine splashed by the children getting in and out of the pool. So a compromise of flagstone and grass was arrived at.

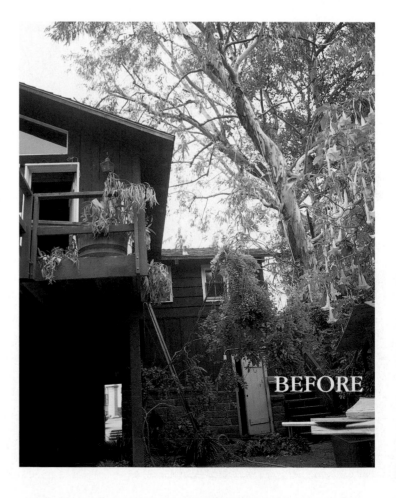

BEFORE

AFTER

inspiration

Above: I had slipcovers made to cover the teak chaise. The bright striped pink fabric is further evidence of my inspiration from the colors of the garden.

P A I N T

Broadly speaking, there are three kinds of paint:

- Matte: the flat paint used to paint interior walls.

- Semi-gloss: for baseboards and trim, and for kitchens and bathrooms, where the paint is exposed to steam and moisture.

- Gloss: too shiny for indoor use, but good for front doors and some exterior trim.

All paint should be applied to a clean, primed surface.
The choices of colors are immense:

- Paint colors look different on walls from how they seem on charts, so paint a sample strip before buying enough paint for the job.

- White has as many variations as other colors. When you are planning to paint a room white, you probably don't want a pure white, unless you like a hospital effect.

- Linen white gives you a white that is not too cold.

- Paint shops will mix colors to your specifications and their computer-assisted processes give an almost infinite range. Remember that custom-mixed colors cannot be returned or exchanged.

My largest investment was in painters and white paint. Although painting the interior and exterior wood took away from the original nature of the house, it was totally necessary to cover it with coats and coats of white paint. On the first day of renovation, the painters arrived: Sergio and his loyal—and appropriately white-uniformed—crew were to be there for many weeks. Before they started to paint they carefully peeled back the wisteria and jasmine so that the plants wouldn't be damaged. Then they prepared and primed the wood. Then they painted. The wood was porous and drank in coat after coat after coat of white paint. Other workmen came and went, but Sergio was there until the very end, even a little after.

Opposite: After gallons of white paint, even on the wicker-front cabinets, light was born. I chose not to have curtains in this room; privacy is not an issue since the house is enclosed by trees. I love the inside-out feeling—except when a raccoon is peering in at me.

The garden was home to many lovely plants, bushes, and trees—as well as to the "blackout" eucalyptus, whose leaves killed the grass and clogged the pool drains, and the "rats' ladder" ivy that covered and strangled house and garden alike. Tree ferns, catalpa, old-fashioned roses, morning glories, honeysuckle, wisteria, heavy, sweet-scented jasmine, and angel's trumpets were revealed in the clearing process. They were lovingly pruned and cared for by Laura, my landscape gardener, who had worked with previous owners and had known the property for more than fifteen years.

Much of the area surrounding the garden had been laid with red brick; although the brick itself was old and lovely, it was too dark, and reluctantly I took much of it out. Fortunately, I was able to find a use for the discarded bricks in the smaller paths that lead from the garden to the main house and guest house. Pale, blond flagstone, quarried locally, was installed around and right up to the edge of the pool.

Above: A pink nightstand with deeper pink flowers.

gardening

Above: A quilted glass vase. Painted pink on the inside to give dull color.

Opposite: My favorite task of the week: in my garden on Wednesday mornings. My vases and flowers are assembled before I begin arranging.

AFTER

The Pool

The pool itself was full of dirty, stagnant water, which had to be drained. Then a team of men—dozens of them, it seemed—chipped away the old and damaged black plaster. It took forever, but finally they were done, and then it was replastered. I chose my own mix of Italian glass mosaic tiles for the border. The finished pool became a big, bright oasis of turquoise right in the middle of the grounds. There is no getting away from its influence, and the color has even begun to creep into the house—I now have in the living room an exquisite chandelier with turquoise drops as well.

Moving the brick, laying the flagstones, and renovating the pool were long, hard, labor-intensive tasks. But it is worth mentioning that this is not a horror story: I had good workmen, I knew what I wanted, and they knew what they were doing. Kevin, my contractor, says, "You don't change your mind much, do you?" That is one of the ways I keep my costs down.

I also save time and money by applying two other simple rules: A quick decision is not necessarily the least good one; and it is not necessary to look at all 5,001 available choices before deciding. If I like the first choice well enough, I take it.

Opposite: I replaced the brick surround of the pool. Although the brick was great, it was too dark. Blond flagstone gave the area around the pool new life. I also replaced the large dark blue Spanish tiles in the pool and spa with small pale blue, turquoise, and pale pink Italian glass tiles. The pool and spa had been lined with black cement, which had to be chipped away before it could be re-cemented. Since the whole house looks out onto it, I wanted the pool to be light.

My Bathroom

When you start to redo a house you immediately become the recipient of plenty of advice, most of it bad. In no area of the house was it so generously offered as in the renovation of my bathroom. My bathroom adjoins my bedroom, so there was a general feeling that it should become more dramatically en suite, that I should rip down walls and build a big, glamorous bathroom, with a separate bath and shower stall, and plenty of closet space. And while I was about it, I should move either the basin or the window, since it was apparently out of the question to have a bathroom with no looking glass over the basin.

This was not what I wanted. I have always dreamed of a pure white bathroom—a *small* pure white tiled bathroom. There are many kinds of subway tiles, which are used in tunnels and are rectangular rather than square; I wanted the ones with the most authentic feel. I paid a little bit extra for some with a nice glaze, with small irregularities in the white dye and in the cutting. They have a handmade feel. The floor tiles are hexagonal and matte white; they come on sheets, each tile about one inch square. I had them installed without a border.

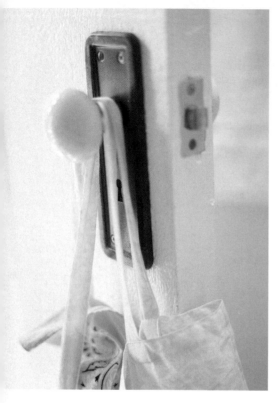

Detail: Hexagonal Ceramic tile

for Master Bathroom

Above: I like the elegance of porcelain, and although the before door handle was the original, I exchanged it for a porcelain handle I liked even better. I was lucky to find enough matching door handles for the whole house. It is unusual to find so many of the same kind, but it's nothing to get hung up on—mix and match a little.

Opposite: The redone bathroom has the look and feel of a renovated bathroom rather than a remodeled one. This is accomplished by using materials and pieces that aren't too slick. The hexagonal floor tile has a matte finish, and the subway wall tile has subtly irregular edges. The bath is simple and has no fussy details. There are no built-in cabinets here and the bathroom is narrow, so the shallow chest-of-drawers is a must. It has to hold all toiletries.

456

terry cl
sho

linen roll-up shade

use mirrors
to add light

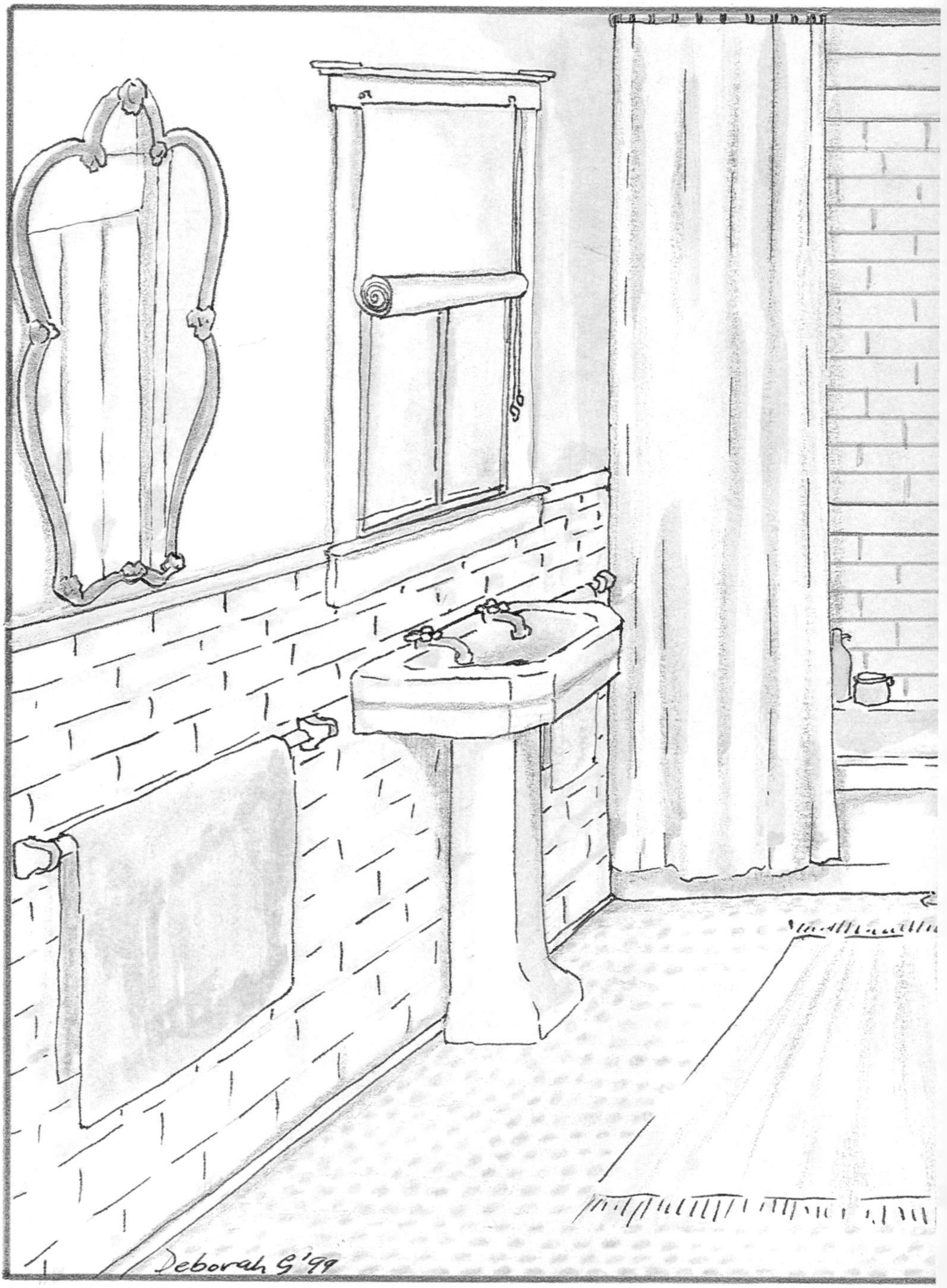

mix old and
new towel bars

subway tile
half-way down
below dado vail

Deborah G '99

simple white, cotton
rug

MASTER

th
~~~er curtain

Install bath

mirrors to be
varied in shape

look for
ways to
make up for
no built-in
storage space
e.g. roomy chest

replace
toilet

BATHROOM

white
hexagonal floor tile
(see detail)

AFTER

accessories

BEFORE

The other decisions I made about my bathroom were equally simple, equally willful. I kept within the four walls that I had inherited. Instead of moving the basin or the window, I installed a makeup mirror on an arm. There are two other looking glasses in the bathroom, one large and plain, the other pretty, but both useful.

I spent some time on bathroom accessories—toilet-roll holders, towel racks, hooks for bathrobes and nightgowns. Hooks and racks were very important, since there was no closet or cupboard for the abundance of soaps and towels that I like to be visible—I don't want them stuffed in a linen cupboard outside the room.

Above: We gutted the bathroom next to my bedroom

Opposite: My trademark luxurious white towel stack, mixing old porcelain and functional repro chrome racks. Again, since there is no cupboard space, stacking is a must.

For these accessories and the fixtures (toilet, bath, basin) as well as the hardware (faucets, racks, hooks), I chose a combination of the authentic originals and the new made-after-classics designs. I bought from several sources: authentic items at Liz's Hardware and classic household reproductions from Restoration Hardware (see Resource Guide). The toilet-roll and soap holders came from the tile shop, since they were a classic design in white tile. If you are starting a bathroom from scratch and you have the luxury, it is well worth creating recesses to house these fixtures. And if, as I was, you are working with a small space, each and every one of those inches that jut out into the room make a difference, so if you can inset these fixtures, it does help quite a bit.

I gave a lot of time and thought to getting the bath, basin, and toilet right. I had only five and a half feet in which to fit the bath—a small space by American standards, but I wanted to work with what I had. I bought the simplest white porcelain bath, and added a six-dollar chrome rod and a terry-cloth shower curtain. The toilet, a good plain design, came from my local plumbing store.

Above: The overflow of beauty products on glazed subway-style tile. Without being too rigid, I try to buy products that fit my color palette. Always flowers in unexpected spaces.

Opposite: These three lovely turquoise glass pots with lids—I bought them at different times—are handy containers for bathroomy things. Among all the sterile white, accessories are an important source of color.

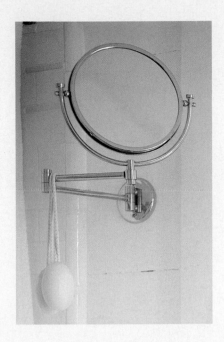

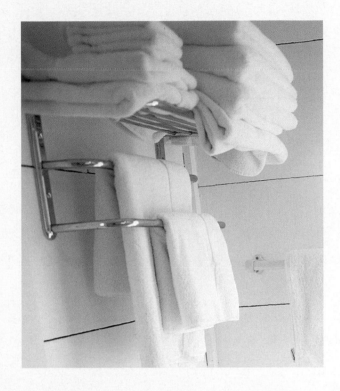

The basin took a little more time. For a moment I even considered building a vanity and dropping a basin into it, for a little surface and storage space. But what I really wanted was what I think of as a New York hotel sink: big and simple. Then I went so far as to take an old sink on approval from a salvage store, but it seemed too tedious to restore and rid it of its old stains. Also, a mixer spout—with both the hot and cold water in one stream—is one of the contemporary luxuries I rather like, so I decided on a new but classic design for the basin itself. For the taps it was a little—but only a *little*—more complicated. My plumber combined authentic porcelain taps with modern plumbing fittings. (I did have to work through my aesthetic needs with the plumber, but now I understand he has started to inflict my neuroses on his other clients.)

PLUMBING

Things to remember when renovating plumbing:

- Be open to mixing old and new. Combining the outward and visible part of an old faucet with a new and efficient plumbing fitting is not a big deal. You can, of course, use the old plumbing fixture that matches your faucet, but why take the chance when new plumbing is more reliable, and it's really only the taps that need to be aesthetically pleasing?

- Old fixtures can be found at salvage companies and flea markets. There is a wonderful choice of lettering and design: sometimes the whole faucet is porcelain, sometimes only the little plate that labels it hot or cold (if you buy French porcelain, remember that C is for chaud, which means hot, not cold!). To find a salvage company, look in the Yellow Pages or telephone your Chamber of Commerce.

- You will also need a soldering company, which your plumber can probably recommend, to solder the faucet handle to the new fixture. Even when this has been done you may need an Allen key to tighten the handle every few months. This is the kind of chore I don't resent— it's well worth the bother. I like to do little things around my house, for my house.

The cost of renovating my bathroom simply, but exactly how I wanted it, was not great by today's standards. It came within the ten thousand dollars I had budgeted for it. The tiles cost three thousand, and all together the bath, basin, and toilet cost fifteen hundred; the remainder was spent on labor and bits and pieces.

Above: Good soap, a luxury I don't scrimp on, in a simple scallop shell.

Opposite: My plumber came to understand my aesthetics. The base of the faucet is new, but we removed the slick handles and replaced them with old taps. This way we got functional new plumbing without losing the beauty of the old handles.

Without being compulsive about it, I try to
choose cosmetics (they sit under a Murano looking
glass on the narrow chest-of-drawers that used to be
in Lily's room) and everyday utilitarian bathroom
products in colors that will look good in my all-white
bathroom. I always place small vases of flowers on the
chest-of-drawers and by the basin. The hard, white
surface of the bathroom is softened by the tablecloth
that in a moment of belated modesty I used as an
interim curtain, sticking it between the sashes of the
window. It worked so well that it still hangs there.

One of the luxuries I enjoy is a fresh bath mat
on the floor, and I like to change mine twice a day. So
I have to allow for a large supply of mats on the rack
and, of course, for a large hamper.

I kept the lighting that came with the bathroom—basic track lighting with big cans, but I
changed the cans to small ones with halogen bulbs
and added a dimmer switch. There are, of course,
plenty of candles.

Opposite: My fancy Italian Murano looking glass, one of three mirrors in this
small space, all with different uses and looks. The rustic chest-of-drawers was
once used to hold the dollhouse in Lily's bedroom (you can see it in my previous book, *Rachel Ashwell's Shabby Chic Treasure Hunting and Decorating
Guide*).

My Bedroom

There is a little step between my bathroom and my bedroom. The house has many little steps, most of them between rooms, and initially my contractor and (for far longer) the advice-givers thought I should get rid of most of them and level off the house in some way, to smooth the transitions between rooms. But I like my steps, and think one should guard against smoothing the character out of a house. I don't want to take any of the life out of my life with unnecessary smoothing-out or the impersonal qualities of technology. There are several time- and energy-saving devices—an intercom, a more convenient outdoor lighting switch—for which I have chosen not to dip into my renovation budget; having to walk up a couple of steps or across the garden to open the front door do not seem like hardships to me. All our technological equipment is kept in the guest-house room we use for an office, and I don't have a television in my bedroom.

Below: The rumpled bed is complemented by the formal elegance of this French chair, with faded and dusty pink quilted upholstery and a worn gold-leaf carved frame—the Shabby and the Chic. The temporary curtain panel is simply thumbtacked onto the window frame; it was too long so I doubled over the top—no big deal. Whenever I think of putting up something more permanent, I can't visualize anything I would like better.

The soffit was built to cover the beam that is directly over my bed. My mother was concerned of the feng shui implications of having a beam over my head, afraid it would stifle my energy. The Chinese needlepoint copy of an Aubusson rug is lightweight and can be folded up like a throw when my daughter practices dance or when I have an exercise session.

I had this wardrobe built for me. There was no closet space in the room and I felt the French armoire needed to be the focus of attention, so I asked a carpenter to build something that would blend into the woodwork. I feel an open closet should be tidy and pleasing to the eye; a cluttered closet feels like a cluttered mind.

I disregarded the suggestions that I should have a walk-in closet. The room is certainly big enough, but I much preferred the creamy, delicately carved armoire I found on a shopping-and-searching trip to Summerland, in Southern California. I use it for sweaters and assorted clothing, and it also houses my sound system—there is even a convenient drawer for CDs. I guiltily had to cut off the back for the stereo equipment to fit.

There is enough space in my bedroom for two fancy armoires, but this is one of the many examples of less being more. Instead, for approximately the same amount of money, I had a wardrobe made to order, so plain that it melts away into the white wall.

Reading Corner
for
Master Bedroom

Above: The ornate French armoire houses bulky sweaters and stereo equipment. This is a typical example of how important it is to know your measurements: the crown molding of the armoire just fits under the beams of the ceiling. I like the contrast between the grandeur of this regal piece and the plain beamed ceiling.

Opposite: A quiet work area. I am careful not to bring work into my room, but some floral artwork pages are allowed.

478

conceal bad Feng Shui' beam
over bed

chai

MASTER BEDROOM ~ January 1999

faded needlepoint Aubosson rug

be upholstered - or slip-covered as alternative

built-in wardrobe with sliding - not open out - doors

keep original stain on floor

Deborah G. '99

Top right: Lily, telling me something very important.

Middle right: We added a subtle rope trim to give the wardrobe a little definition.

Right: I can't bear cluttered closets. If my shoes are messy, it's probably time to get rid of some.

comfort

My bedroom is the largest room in the house, with the most floor space, and for a smaller family would probably be the living room. But with only two other bedrooms, for my children, I need this space as my own room. I looked for a carpet large enough to fill the space but lightweight enough to be easily moved, since the floor is the logical place for me to exercise and for my daughter to do her dance practice.

My bed is the central point of the room. I have no headboard, but lots of pillows and an absolutely necessary mosquito net suspended overhead. One way or another, the bed is home for a lot of fabric. So I added a small, elegant pink chair by the window, whose fine-lined deli-cacy balances the soft casualness of the bed. The windows are covered with lace panels, again held in place with thumbtacks; there is not a rod, pole, or curtain ring in the whole room. The white walls are bare except for my "Humility" plaque, about priorities, which was featured in my previous book.

No headboard—I like the simplicity. The mosquito net is vital, but even if it weren't, I love how it looks, open and closed. On a warm day even a duvet or comforter is not necessary. A simple gauzy sheet is pretty and throwaway-chic enough that the bed, even unmade, looks fresh and inviting.

Above: Black-and-white shows clearly how much lovelier less can be. Beautiful textures.

A favorite chair.

The Kitchen

The kitchen is next to the bedroom. Almost too convenient, since at night I can hear the hum and purr from my beautiful glass-front refrigerator. The refrigerator and stove came with the house, and I treasure them. But they come at a price: the fridge is noisy, and the old-fashioned professional catering stove has an intermittently unreliable pilot light. I go back and forth in my mind about replacing them someday.

The kitchen, albeit small, is easy to work in. There is plenty of cupboard space, more than I really need, and that is a luxury. I painted the whole room white—the cabinets, ceiling, and even the overhead copper light-fitting. The food in the glass-front refrigerator provides most of the color in the kitchen. There is fluorescent lighting under all the cabinets, something I would not have put in myself, but since it's there I find it useful. The faucets and the sink I replaced—the simplest I could find.

I also replaced the brown granite slab counter with white-and-light-gray-veined marble. The marble was a major item in my budget: It was important to me to have a kitchen that was not only hygienic and easy to keep really clean but that I also enjoyed being in. I was very careful that the marble should not look too slick and chose a dull finish. There is not enough room in the kitchen to do a lot of anything decor-wise. And the fewer materials I used, the cleaner and smoother the room looked. I carried the marble up the

Opposite: The contents of these cabinets are part of the decoration for this living space.

487

wall to the cabinets' bottom, to make a splashboard. But again, this work was much more of a renovation than a remodel.

The kitchen is not only light and functional, but it is also part of the decor of the living room. I imagine that if the original intention of the house was for my bedroom to be the living room, then our present living room would be the dining room, which may explain why part of our living room wall is composed of the kitchen cabinets. The cabinets open into the kitchen and still have their original, slightly rippled handmade glass— the subtle imperfections are striking and charming, and they are always among the first details my guests notice. The china I keep in them is an important part of the balance of color in the room. Below the marble counter, the wood-frame cupboards have wicker inlays, which were rattan-colored but are now washed in the same white as the cabinets. I was very lucky to have found both storage areas in such serviceable condition: Replacing or even significantly renovating kitchen cabinets is a surprisingly serious endeavor—not one that should be taken lightly, nor one that can be accomplished inexpensively. Before deciding to rip out old cabinets and start afresh, consider altering the existing ones to suit your taste and needs.

I store my table linens in these lower cupboards, and it is always a pleasure for me to open the door and see my white and floral linens. They are not stacked formally or even always very tidily, but the result is always pretty. I try to make sure that any cupboard I open anywhere in the house gives me similar pleasure.

Love, love this fridge and the display of products, but I am thinking of replacing it, since, sadly, it is a little too noisy, being too close to my bedroom.

Above: Tweety. Bohemian color against the white.

Opposite: The kitchen. Everything, even the front of the dishwasher, is painted white. I added marble and new faucets. I like the industrial feel.

details

Above: Today's faucets—I can barely believe the choices. For me, however, once again classic and simple (which also happen to be the cheapest).

Opposite: Carrera marble honed to a blunt, straight edge, not bullnosed into a thick, rounded edge that gives the illusion of bulk. Many people today have shiny countertops that are a little too slick for my taste. Some warn that the porous nature of marble causes it to retain stains, especially if you remove the shiny surface. But I haven't had a problem.

The beautiful rests on the foundations of the necessary.

—Ralph Waldo Emerson

Above top: I like the way the central pattern slips under the rim to join the border pattern.

Above: An inviting cake plate.

Opposite: Even opening the dishwasher should be a joyful experience. All plates, cups, and saucers should be pieces you love to see. Mismatched is all right; ugly is not.

The Living Room & Dining Area

Every window in my house has a view, and one wall of my living room is entirely glass—windows, a French door, and the entrance door. The glass wall brings the colors of the pool and the garden into the house. The turquoise drops on the chandelier are the same color as the pool; before installing it, once I would have unpicked every turquoise drop and replaced it with clear glass, and I probably would have tried to do something about the gold paint as well. Now I leave it all as is, thanks to the colorful inspirations that surround me. The rest of the room is lit by sconces, lamps, and candles.

The living room is sparsely decorated: just a few paintings and some family photographs on the walls and propped around; the room depends on the outdoors for its decor. As the seasons change the flowers in the garden, I change my slipcovers in the living room. It is the best room in the world for a rainy day. And, of course, there are no curtains.

Above: The before living room. The wood was dark, dark, dark, and I was grateful for the skylights. A few wood lovers disapproved of painting natural wood white—oh, well!

My spring slipcovers: a muted monochromatic teal floral pattern. With them, an unusual teal alabaster lamp. The slipcovers, the lamp, and the flowers can provide subtle but significant changes for the season.

White linen slipcovers replaced the white denim I lived with for many years. My children are now old enough to handle the more sophisticated linen. My coffee table is an old oak door, painted white, which sits on inexpensive Home Depot turned wooden legs. A piece of glass creates a smooth surface over the carved top.

w h i m s y

Above: A detail of an old door we use as a table; I painted it and put glass on top.

Opposite: Twinkle whimsy. Once I would have taken the turquoise crystals off this chandelier before I installed it, but the color of their sparkle is a reflection of the swimming pool outside.

The curtainless view of the garden is not the only instance of the immediacy of nature. Sometimes at night a convention of raccoons dances on the roof, and even more noisily on the skylights. The raccoons are far from bashful, and I warn my guests to keep the door of the guest house firmly shut unless they want to find a family of utterly cute but sharp-toothed and possibly rabid raccoons cuddled up beside them.

The beautiful wide-plank wooden floors in the living room—indeed, throughout the house—were a wonderful surprise, and in nearly perfect condition: The irregular-width planks weren't missing or damaged or loose, and I didn't have to pull up carpeting or linoleum (then scrape off glue, then sand, then stain, and then finish); I barely needed to apply a new coat of wax.

Similarly, the walls and ceilings gave me no trouble: no wallpaper to steam off, no sheetrocking or spackling to repair major cracks or holes, just coats and coats of white paint. There's no molding—this is much more of a cabin than a cottage—and so I avoided another potential headache. And although the beautiful sash windows were hard to open, they didn't need serious attention: I merely renewed the sashes to ease opening, and replaced the locks and screens for a uniform look. This was only a couple days' work, instead of the major overhaul (and huge expense) that old wood windows often demand.

Opposite: The teal floral chair from my living room.

The Guest House

My guest house, minus the raccoons, is light, pretty, and multifunctional, and is built over the garage, which includes the laundry room and the infamous tunnel to the garden. One climbs a flight of exterior wooden stairs to a large, sunny deck, which is level with the upper branches of the surrounding bushes and trees—only the eucalyptus towers above. The deck is a lovely place for my guests to sit during the day, to enjoy the sun and breathe in the scent of the sweet-smelling angel's trumpets and jasmine; or at night, to look at the sky through the eucalyptus branches, pleasantly aware of the many sweet-smelling plants below.

BEFORE

506

AFTER

When buying old light fixtures, always have wiring and plugs checked and replaced at a local lamp or lighting store. I get this type of white cording and plug instead of the standard dark brown plastic wire, a small detail that makes all the difference.

MAINTENANCE OF WOODEN FLOORS

I infinitely prefer a waxed floor to one sealed with polyurethane. A waxed floor takes a little more work but is more than worth it. Instead of that high-gloss nail-polish finish of polyurethane, the floor looks rich, beautiful, and will become even more lovely with age.

The care of polished floors is largely a matter of common sense:

• Mop up anything you spill right away, and don't allow potted plants to sit on the floor—their dripping water will stain and grain the wood.

• Use doormats to limit the incoming dirt, and don't allow grit to get tracked into the room.

• Vacuum regularly, and in between thorough cleanings, use a soft brush or dry mop to keep the floor shiny.

• Have the floors professionally waxed and buffed twice a year.

Opposite: Pink dresser with mirror. Usually I would replace the handles with glass, but in this case I felt the dark handles provided a little masculinity that echoes the darker floors.

The guest house is well built—it too has good bones. It is solidly made of quality wood and has a fine brick fireplace in the bedroom. The outer room serves as an office, and the bedroom serves not only as a music room, but also, thanks to a super-comfortable sofa bed and a wardrobe rack (there are no closets in the guest house), as welcoming guest quarters. The floors are made of the same magnificent wood as the main house, and here too the wide-plank boards do not match in width. I am proud of how lovely and inviting the guest house is, especially since I made few changes, working with what came with the house. Although, as usual, I didn't stint on the white paint.

Above: A cashmere cardigan with a fake fur collar. It feels sumptuous. A set of four green velvet hangers tied with green silk ribbon. I always keep an eye open for pretty old hangers at flea markets, thrift shops, and garage sales.

Opposite: Lack closet space? A wardrobe rack can do the job. And if your clothes are of a focused and pretty palette and you choose yummy hangers, it can be decorative in itself.

512

Things to consider when buying a house:

- Buy a house for what it is, so you can restore it, not remodel it.

- Don't be bullied by so-called experts.

- Don't feel you have to see 5,001 examples if you really like the first one.

- Having something custom-made sometimes doesn't cost more than buying it, especially if it is something with specific measurements or function—a piece for a narrow hallway, for example.

- Less is more. (One great armoire in my bedroom is better than two.)

Opposite: Shades of pink loosely arranged in a darker pink vase.

2

LEAVING IT

ALONE &

SURPRISING

MYSELF

When you have chosen and bought the house you want, it is important to take a little time to look with an open mind at what is now yours and make an effort to shed preconceived ideas. I surprised myself by how pleased I became with some of the so-called compromises I had made—*after* I'd had a little time to live with them.

I didn't want white, white, white furniture in the living area of my guest house. I wanted more color, to be more eclectic here. A profusion of throw pillows helps to achieve that. The sofa and the little side table came from my last house (and my first book!). We removed the exterior of a wall-length cedar closet and kept the interior fittings for shelves. I left the trim of the windows dark here, to break up the white everywhere else. Again, there is no need for curtains. All the windows look out onto a private garden, and such lovely foliage.

A flowerless home is a soulless room to my way of thinking; but even one solitary little vase of a living flower may redeem it.

—Vita Sackville-West

Once I made my list of essential changes, I had to review the house again, deciding how much of my wish list I could afford and choosing some of the compromises I would have to make. Perhaps the largest—but one that bothered me very little—was that I was not able to use some of the rooms as they had been originally intended: my bedroom was intended to be the living room; Jake's room, although certainly large enough to be a bedroom, had probably been the library (the walls are lined with shelves), and now it doubles as both Jake's bedroom and a throughway to Lily's room and the children's bathroom.

Opposite: In my guest-house kitchenette. The first time I saw this orange tile, I thought it would be the first thing to go. But after seeing it every now and again (remember, it's my guest house), I decided it might be fun to just leave alone.

Three of my choices to leave things alone involved the guest house, which is partly a coincidence. But partly, these compromises were made because it is easier to live with what isn't quite your taste when it happens to be in rooms you use the least. The decision was most certainly not because I thought "It's only the guest house."

The guest house is composed of a deck, two rooms, a kitchenette, and a bathroom. The front room had a huge walk-in closet made of cedar that ran the full length of the room. I didn't want to use up all that space, so I had the outer wall removed. Once that was gone, the economical solution seemed to be to leave most of the built-in interior. Rather than go to the expense of demolishing the fittings and refinishing the wall, I adapted what was left.

Now I have a small shelved cupboard for household cleaners and storage. Next to it are open shelves, which I pass several times a day, so I use them for inspiration and keep fabrics, lamps, mirrors, and parasols on them—and sometimes, hanging from a shelf, a colorful item of flea-market clothing. Beside these open shelves are some drawers. I don't really need them, but since the guest house doubles as my office (as well as Lily's music room, for practicing piano), I find a use for them. Along the greater part of the wall is a counter that we use for computers and other office equipment. The counter is too high, but rather than go to the expense of lowering it, I bought tall stools. And all these fittings—cupboards, shelves, drawers, and counter—are made of best-quality, pleasantly scented cedar.

The guest-house bathroom lends itself to whimsy and accents that I might not want to live with or see every day. For me, yellow flowers!! Once in a while it's fun.

things kept

The inexpensive stained brown wood surrounding the windows in the guest bathroom was one of the rare areas to escape the white paintbrush. I felt like breaking up the white, and the brown border frames a lovely view of tall, closely planted trees.

The guest-house kitchenette countertop is made up of small, oblong orange tiles. When I bought the house, I imagined they would be among the first to go, but after a while I came to enjoy their cheerful energy. When it was time to redo the kitchenette, I left them as they were and painted the rest of the kitchen—except for the brown-framed window directly above them—my usual white.

The guest bathroom came with an eclectic range of materials: brass fittings, heavily veined gray marble countertops, a white porcelain basin decorated with a pink floral motif, blue-gray bath and shower tiles with intermittent pink detail. And a bidet. None of which I would have chosen, but with the woodwork and bathroom closets painted white, I have become fond of the way this room looks.

There are perhaps fifteen old-fashioned copper lantern-style electric sconces on the house and in the garden. I thought I would keep them for the time being but replace them later; now I have become quite attached to them.

Above: The bidet came with the house, and I kept it.

Opposite: A basin in the guest-house bathroom. I would never have chosen a pink-decorated sink or a marble with as much gray vein as this, but I was happy to leave it alone, and now I have become rather fond of the textures and detail. A nice variation on my white.

I can see now that having to wait a little—to relax into a new house, to live with objects or arrangements that might not be my first choice—is often a blessing. The restoration of a house deserves the investment of thought, consideration, and time, as well as work and money.

Fortunately, budgetary reasons prevented me from some alterations I was advised to make—most of them, it turned out, pertaining to convenience or saving time. But I like to spend a little time on my house—my *home*—and I enjoy strolling through the garden in the evening to switch on the outside lights, even though it would be quicker, and more efficient, to have had the switch moved to the living room. I also like walking through my garden during the day to answer the front door, although I could, for a price, have had an intercom installed.

I was urged to join the guest house to the main house, and I knew this would add to the resale value of the house. Although resale value should be a consideration when making such a decision, it should not be a priority, and my decision not to join the two houses was largely budgetary as well. As a result, the main house has become the more peaceful house; we eat, sleep, and talk there. The guest house tends to be where activity takes place—it houses the computers, the baby-grand piano, and the only television. It is where I work and where Lily practices the piano.

Above: There are about fifteen of these lanterns dotted about outside. Another example of something that, were I starting from scratch, I might not have bought, but innocuous enough to let be.

That the television is in the guest house ensures that I am not seduced into watching more television than I think healthy. It also tends to make viewing somewhat of an occasion—such as when the whole family and our friends assemble to watch the Oscars. Sometimes, when it rains, I wish I had joined the two houses; but more often I enjoy the time spent between them, feeling the sun on my skin, seeing and smelling flowers and plants on the way. Then—and that is most of the time—I am glad I left well enough alone.

Things to consider when leaving it alone:

• Live with what you've bought for a little while. Relax into it.

• Don't change your mind more than you have to.

• Choose what you are willing to compromise on.

Above: Flea-market table with glass top. An alabaster lamp base with a Shabby Chic linen shade.

Right: I lucked out with the existing glass doorknobs in the guest bathroom. They're sweet.

EVERY EXIT IS AN
ENTRY SOMEWHERE ELSE.

—*Tom Stoppard*

3

HALLWAYS,
NOOKS &
CRANNIES

I enjoy the spa, but I would never have gone to the expense of installing one; a cedar-lined sauna wouldn't have been on my list either. So I was fortunate to find both luxuries already included. Although I have hung colorful pareos in the sauna, I rarely use it, and Lily has made it her special nook.

There are two hallways of which I am particularly fond: one in the main house between the living room, the kitchen, and my bedroom, and the other in the guest house. In my hallways, the light often comes from several directions, and so they are shadowy and beautiful, particularly in the hall off the kitchen, which I'm constantly walking through. When we moved into this house, the telephone was in this six-foot-long passage, between the kitchen and my bedroom; I left it there, and now spend more time here than I would wish, sitting on one of the little steps that didn't get smoothed out, with a notepad on my knee. But because the space is so pretty, I don't mind lingering.

Above: The telephone reaches everywhere; sadly, necessity comes with the territory of owning a business.

Opposite: Cedar-lined and cedar-scented, the sauna doubles as Lily's playhouse.

Opposite: These things are usually somehow tied into a new product or design I am working on for Shabby Chic. Sometimes an item may sit here for quite some time, until one day I see it in a certain way, and it becomes my inspiration.

539

a perfect nook

Opposite: A perfect spot to hold all the things needed at various times for my nearby dining table. Again, a lovely place to glance. Nothing is ever here long.

Some of the cupboards in the kitchen are high, and Lupe (my housekeeper and much, *much* more) isn't very tall. When I realized we would need a ladder and didn't have anywhere to store it in the kitchen, I found a pretty green one and gave it a place beside the telephone, across from my parakeet Tweety's freestanding cage and my nonoffice desk in the hallway.

The guest house hallway is a little longer, about eight feet long. It joins the guest bedroom/music room to the bathroom and also to a secondary staircase. It is the perfect place for a quiet watercolor painting, a laundry hamper, and one of my inspirational notice boards—covered with pieces of fabric, drawings, scraps of paper. I try to arrange my house so that there are as many places as possible to inspire me. My hallways are among these places.

Above: Hallways and thoroughfares are part of the house too, not to be left out of the overall decor. I spend hours talking on the telephone on the floor in this hallway. The green ladder and the birdcage cover serve two necessary functions but also add a lovely touch of color.

Opposite: Every cupboard should hold things of beauty or function. I allow for one junk drawer or cupboard in my house. Otherwise, whenever I open a cupboard it should be like Christmas, beautiful and sumptuous. It doesn't need to be organized perfectly.

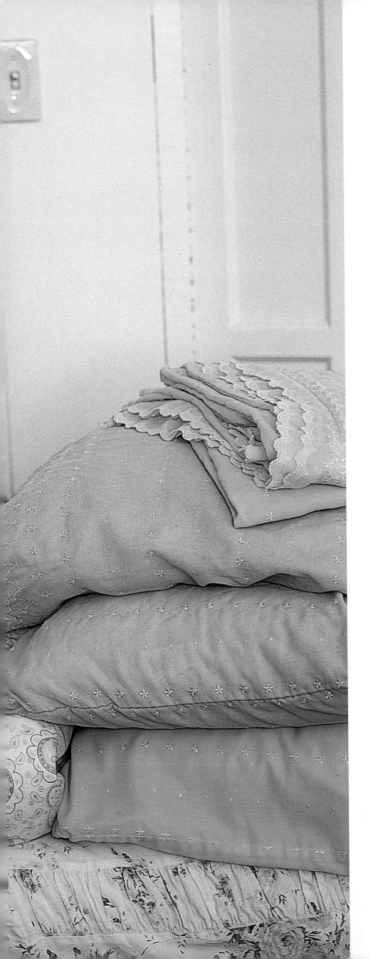

It is a mistake to ignore hallways, or to treat them as meaningless dead space between rooms. The sum total of hallway space may be greater than the largest single room in any house; you may, as I do, spend as much time in hallways as in the rooms proper. So keep your eyes open for small, useful pieces of furniture that can make good use of this space: a narrow bookshelf, a small end table, a lonely single chair. Little pieces can have an intimate charm that more imposing pieces could never match, and can also be quite inexpensive and easy to get home and move around.

Left: Some things are so pretty that even when not in use, I don't want to pack them away in a cupboard. I like to see this overflowing stack of duvets and pillows.

545

Even better than simply adding unnecessary furniture is finding beautiful examples of completely useful items that you don't want to hide: My pale blue laundry hamper couldn't be a better color, and I'm glad the bathroom can't accommodate it; it would be a shame to hide the lovely green stepladder in a utility closet, which I don't have. Both items serve important purposes, and serve those purposes all the better because they're attractive.

There are several nooks and crannies in the living room. Since the living room is not large and also serves as the dining room, useful and attractive storage space is important. Between the fireplace and the door to Jake's room is an alcove with room for a small table, where I store china close to the dining table. I use everything pretty I own; I don't see the point of having cupboards full of "special" things gathering dust. If I don't use something, it goes out. I either give it to a friend, or Lupe finds it a new home where it will be appreciated—and used. This way my cupboards and closets are not overfilled. When I open them, I look at their contents with pleasure, not despair or guilt.

Opposite: Hallways often catch the best light and shadows in a house. Here is a perfect example of a simply beautiful spot. A path well trodden is often as important as the destination. Painted wicker laundry basket: the color and condition were perfect as I found this, but I did line the inside with muslin.

I have at last found a resting place for a sconce I brought with me from my last house (as seen in my first book): a shelf on the wall just beside Jake's room. It lights Jake's painting of two plums and a bowl. I propped a couple of favorite flea-market floral paintings beside it, and in its own way, this shelf became a small nook.

Above: Every nook and hallway deserves good lighting. I'm always on the lookout for great old sconces. But I only use them if there is preexisting wiring; it's way too much work to wire a sconce into a finished wall.

Opposite: Proportionately wrong, perhaps, to have a light fixture of this size here, but next to my son's painting seemed to me the perfect place for this pale green wooden sconce.

The smallest cranny is in the children's bathroom. Hung on the wall is a lovely flea-market cabinet, the door of which is inlaid with an old looking glass. It has well-proportioned shelves and little drawers for Lily's hair ornaments, like a treasure box in a secret garden.

Above: A teenage girl's drawer. Fun.

Opposite: A bathroom cupboard: old, refurbished, painted white, distressed, now elegant with its oval looking glass, and luxurious with the pampering cosmetics and toiletries inside. They are all, in an uncontrived way, pretty colors and pleasing shapes.

Though we travel the world over to find the beautiful, we must carry it with us or we find it not.

—RALPH WALDO EMERSON

4

SLEEPING &
SNOOZING

My house is a hive of activity during most of the day: The children and their friends are in and out; Lupe keeps the house clean and battles the waves of laundry that each day brings; I often work at home: and now that I have a television show to fit into my already tight schedule, the energy level in the house is often high.

And so, of course, is the stress level. I cope with this by having a series of little havens around the house and garden, places where I can rest, think, read, do quiet work, and even nap occasionally.

If I need ten minutes during the day to restore my energy, I lie on my hammock. The hammock is lined with a feather bed and pillows, both covered in one of my pale floral patterns, and is slung between two sturdy eucalyptus trees. Every year I have these eucalyptus laced (thinned out) to allow the sun and sky into my garden. Their heavy leaves, the bane of the lawn and pool, provide shade as I lie looking at the garden, at times thinking that this is what heaven must be like. The gentle rhythm of the hammock, the hum of the garden, and the scent of the flowers all revive my spirits, and soon I am ready to rejoin the world.

Above: A deviation from my pinks: the cool teal colors in some of my new bedding designs.

Opposite: The most inviting snoozing place for me; I feel grounded by the rhythm of the hammock, lined with a feather bed and a large down throw pillow, and the solid size of the huge eucalyptus trees. The environment makes for a perfect nap. Next to the hammock I have a contemporary teak dining table and chairs. I wanted something I didn't have to worry about; it didn't seem like the spot for Shabby Chic worn metal or painted wicker.

The guest house has a large and sunny deck. When I bought the house, the whole deck was lined with bench seating. I expanded part of this banquette with planks to make a platform for a large mattress and cushions, which are covered with a dusty pink waterproof fabric so they can stay outside, and there is also a large patio umbrella nearby. I often spend an afternoon here, thinking and doing quiet work. Sometimes I have a summer nap under some light bedding; if this pleasant time stretches into the evening hours, I add a mosquito net, which serves its true purpose.

Above: Pink tissue-paper flowers, bunched in an unusual blue-and-white plant pot. I found the pot in England.

Opposite: My sun deck. The cushions are covered in a waterproof dusty pink cloth, acts as a good base, and I can leave them outside in all weather.

559

*The future belongs to those who believe in
the beauty of their dreams.*

—ELEANOR ROOSEVELT

Above: A raspberry etched-glass vase, with the perfect mouth for a generous display of berry-red roses.

Opposite: Creating a place to rest. There is something so freeing about the elements of the ocean.

Although the bed in the guest room is a convertible sofa, it is very luxurious. There is no need to compromise on comfort with a sofa bed—it should be just as plush as though one slept on it every night. My guests are here because they are people I care about, and I wouldn't dream of using castoffs or second-rate furniture in my guest quarters. I like my guests to have plenty of soft, *soft* pillows (the arms of the sofa are a bonus, since there are big pillows to stack against them) and pretty sheets.

In the guest bathroom I have lots and lots of fluffy towels and deliciously scented soap, freshly unwrapped before guests arrive. And, of course, flowers are every-where—picked from the garden, given by friends, or bought.

Above: When I dye fabrics at home, there is always an element of surprise in the end result, but my palette is forgiving to different shades of pinks, greens, and blues.

Opposite: A sofa bed doesn't have to be lumpy and uncomfortable. It can and *should* be just as luxurious as any other bed. Here I have extra pillows, all with a pink theme and an accent of turquoise.

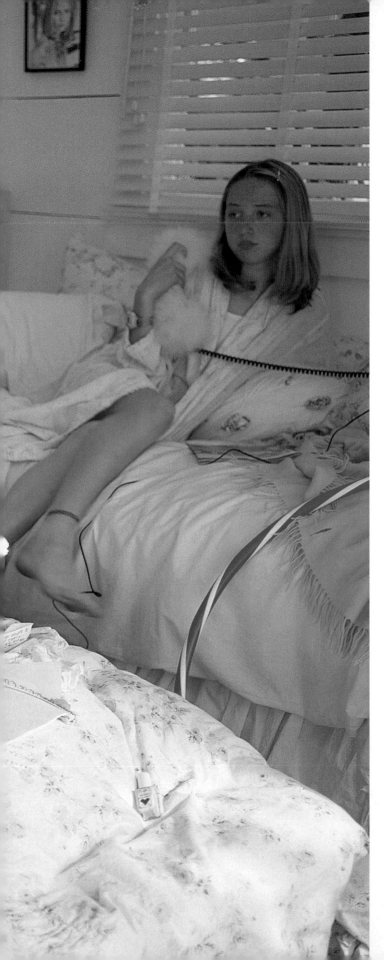

slumber parties

My children are at an age when much of their social life involves sleepovers and, for more special occasions, slumber parties. I love to have my children's social life in the home, and I find slumber parties easy and fun: It is effortless to make them festive and exciting (and it is a comfortable and unobtrusive way for me to get to know their friends). The children provide their own entertainment, and I provide food, refreshments, and plenty of inviting bedding. There is always an abundance of pillows, linens, and comfortable quilts around the house, luxurious without being in any way extravagant. Everything is simple, but it is sumptuous—feather beds and duvets are stacked up in open view on an army-cot spare bed—and it is all durable, washable. The kids and their friends sleep on the sofa bed or sometimes just curl up on a mushy couch with lots of soft, luxurious bedding.

Opposite: A slumber party for my daughter and her friends. Paper forget-me-nots hanging from fishing line give a dreamy effect. A basic army cot is dressed with a luxurious feather bed; sumptuous duvets maintain my standards of comfort and beauty.

dreamy

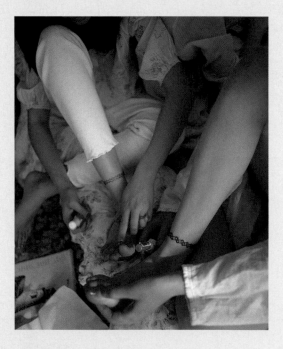

Above left: A fuzzy feathery pink telephone for teenage phone calls.

Opposite: A vintage night jacket—charming.

It is this same abundance of bedding—especially pillows—that enables me to skip the fussiness of a headboard in my own pared-down bedroom and that provides great flexibility with the children's rooms: No matter what their current decorating fascinations, their rooms always share the same comfortable look with the rest of the house.

Opposite: My palace, my dream. Caribbean . . . French . . . rustic . . . and casual sexy elegance.

We are fortunate to live close to the beach—another superb spot to take a nap—and I make sure there is also an abundance of portable, lightweight beach stuff—sarongs, towels, mats. Sometimes at night I can hear the ocean from my bed, and it reminds me that the beach is a peaceful place for quiet times.

Above: I enjoy making a comfortable place to nap on the beach.

Right: Nothing is more angelic than a resting child.

574

But on a rainy night there is no place more inviting to sleep than my own bed. Piles and piles of pillows, eclectic bedding, and a mosquito net suggest an incipient canopy overhead. My bed is neatly but not formally made, so it invites me to plop onto it if I have a few minutes to spare. Maybe to read, meditate, or do nothing.

My bedroom and bathroom are where I like to enjoy scents from my aromatherapy diffuser. I put in a few drops of relaxing lavender—or if I feel the need for calming energy, some eucalyptus—into the dispenser and breathe them in. My sense of touch is satisfied by the comfort I draw from the texture and softness of my bed and furnishings; my sight is fed by the beauty around me. Since the sense of smell is more powerful than the sense of sight, it often draws me back into the past. It would make me happy to think that my children will one day be drawn back into memories of me and our house when they breathe in the scent of lavender.

s o f t n e s s

A beautiful reflection, beautifully framed.

A pile of blue jeans is always a welcome
sight at the foot of my bed. I never know
when I may need them, and Levi's blue is a
favorite color.

I think a black-and-white photograph
shows an uncontrived beauty. Nothing
hiding behind color.

577

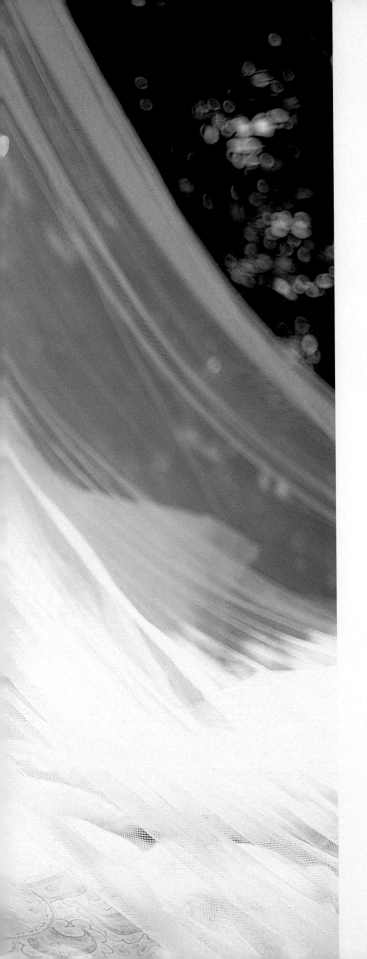

*Nothing happens unless
first we dream.*

—CARL SANDBURG

5

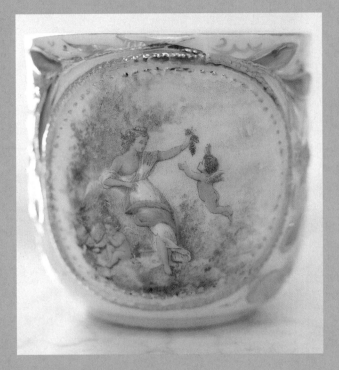

CUPIDS, CHINA
& GIRLS
IN PRETTY
DRESSES

I love to entertain—to be with my family and friends, to use all my pretty china, to dress up a little. I keep entertaining painless and anxiety-free by a mixture of modesty and abundance. In my house there is no "best" china, nothing that I put away for special occasions. When friends come to spend a day or evening, there is just more of it set out. And since nothing matches—although everything looks good together—having enough (or the appropriate) china is not something I ever have to worry about. I do not, if fact, worry about *any* aspect of entertaining. Although I go to some thought and trouble to make everything pleasant, pretty, and celebratory, my first rule of entertaining is not to make myself so anxious that I don't enjoy my guests.

So I know—and set—my limitations. I keep the food I serve simple and choose from menus that can be prepared largely in advance; I put out all the china, silver, and glass that I expect to need and also use it as part of the decoration. And I fill my house with flowers.

Opposite: Beautiful but unmatched—a gaudy teapot, an elegant cup and saucer with a formal frieze pattern, a stack of berry bowls on a stack of assorted plates—more than this party needs, but I like the abundance and choice. The flowers, rescued from a broken stem, float in my silver goblets.

Above: A French Havilland oyster dish. To me it's as fine as a piece of jewelry.

None of this need be particularly expensive, or difficult. I have limited dining space indoors, so I usually have my larger gatherings during the summer and entertain in the garden. I open the French doors and push my dining table between them; on it I place a cold buffet and a profusion of mismatched plates and linen napkins. My guests can serve themselves either from the garden or the living room.

Above: Festive ornamental Peruvian candles.

Opposite: This is as elegant as it gets in my house: gold and white china, silver, linen, and shells on an Indian sari. I like how the sari is so fine that you can see the table through it.

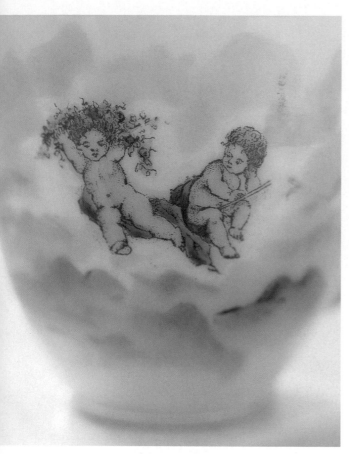

s i m p l e

The food I serve is simple and set out in a manner that makes it attractive. For a summer buffet, I might serve cold meats on a platter, and a variety of breads, salads, and cheeses, with a large fresh-fruit salad. For a smaller winter meal, say for six people eating at the dining table, I may cook chicken with roast potatoes and vegetables. Simple and delicious—I avoid sauces or last-minute preparation during the time I want to spend with my guests. For a tea party, it might be even more simple—tea, hot or iced, and an inexpensive cake, which I decorate with flowers.

The serving dishes, plates, and bowls my friends use have been collected over the years at flea markets, thrift stores, and secondhand shops. Very few of them have cost more than a few dollars: even now it is very rare for me to pay more than fifteen dollars for a plate; a pitcher or jug usually costs between fifteen and fifty dollars; and a really pretty cup and saucer shouldn't be more than twenty-five dollars. If you buy a dinner service that is incomplete, it will be considerably less expensive, and you can mix and match. If you live in a location where there aren't many flea markets or thrift shops, you can sometimes find what you are looking for through a china matching or replacement service (see Resource Guide).

Above: The mark on the back of one of my cupid plates tells me it was made at the turn of the century in Bohemia. I bought each piece at a different time, and they are all different makes. Cupid is shown on these pieces as a sweet, if rather plump, baby; the most recent incarnation of the god of love. In Greek mythology he was Eros, son of Hermes and Aphrodite. The Romans called him Amor, and his parents were Mercury and Venus. In Hellenistic and classical art he was portrayed as a youth or young man. By the later Renaissance he was a small child, and then he became merged with the putti (winged infants).

A table setting is nicely rounded out with mix-and-match antique silver and crystal. Again, buying individual, orphaned pieces is much less expensive—and also much more interesting (not to mention more fun)—than buying full sets. And the inevitable silver-spoon-meets-garbage-disposal confrontation isn't the tragedy it would be if the spoon were from an otherwise intact set.

Although I treasure my china, I use it and the linen napkins (also from flea markets) every day. I take great pleasure drinking from fine bone china and really don't like thick-rim mugs. The plates go in the dishwasher and the napkins in the washing machine. Both of these conveniences tend to take their toll, but I don't mind my napkins becoming thinner and the colors on my plates fading a little.

Sometimes I wash my china by hand, not as a chore but because I want to take an unhurried moment to enjoy it and take pleasure in the things that are part of my house and home. We all have busy lives and I am always grateful that I have help—Lupe, a gardener, and a pool cleaner. Nevertheless, I think it is important not to delegate all the household chores. Certain tasks are necessary so that I can feel I am living my life, caring for my home. Although I don't do it all the time, I like to wash my dishes, dust my house, make the beds; it gives me time to experience and appreciate my home.

Opposite: The box and wrapping of these silver goblets are almost as appealing as the dishes themselves. I like to use them as finger bowls, or to put one with flowers in front of each of my guests as tiny individual floral arrangements.

And there are two exceptions to my "put everything in the dishwasher" rule. My Havilland oyster plates—part of a set, made in Limoges, France, especially for a jeweler—are family treasures. I prefer to wash them by hand; but we do use them for everyday. The other exception is my cupid china collection. I bought each of these pieces at a different time, finding them at flea markets or secondhand shops. When I buy a piece of china the last thing I look for is the mark. But when I have found something I love, and it has a china mark, it is fun and interesting to be able to look up when it was made, where, and by what factory. Good pottery and porcelain bears the maker's mark on its reverse side. The mark may be a name or a cryptic symbol, often both. If you know how to read the mark you will be able to tell where and approximately when it was made. *Kovel's New Dictionary of Marks* (see Resource Guide) is a useful reference. The marks themselves, especially the older ones that seem to have blurred or bled into the glaze, are frequently lovely, and often of my palette. My Havilland oyster dishes are marked, but only one of my cupid plates is.

Before I arrange my table, I choose a theme: it could be a mix of colors, gold and white, or pink, or all white; or it could be all floral; or only cupids. While I am a firm believer in mixing and matching, a table (or even a cupboard) should not become a mishmash of leftover plates and cups.

I also set out flowers. The cost of having them around varies with the season and, of course, with location. Buying flowers in the middle of a California summer costs a great deal less than it would in, say, December in Chicago. In either case, it does not have to be a major extravagance so long as you remember that you don't have to have an enormous amount of flowers for the right effect; you can choose flowers that last, and look after them properly.

A moiré dress. The color, the lace, the ruffles, the pleating—I find it irresistible. Dresses such as this can be bought for pennies.

A tea party. An inexpensive supermarket cake, decorated with flowers. Lots of vases of flowers placed casually off-center. They make for a very special and festive table.

I like to cluster my flower vases, maybe three different sizes set off-center on one table. And when I am serving a sit-down dinner, I like to place one bloom in a bud vase in front of each guest. Bud vases are very cheap, or you can often find a pretty old jar or bottle. I avoid a large centerpiece on the dining table, where it gets in the way of seeing the person opposite you.

The willingness to improvise makes entertaining less expensive and more fun. If you don't have the right kind of tablecloth, find a pretty cloth that has another function—perhaps a curtain; one of my favorite decorating ideas for a table is the use of an Indian sari. I add my flea-market silver, some shells, flower petals, sea glass, marbles. Again a theme, but uncontrived and haphazard. I like to make an individual decoration for each place setting, a whimsical personal arrangement for each guest. The key to a successful individual style is being creative with what you already have.

And what to wear while entertaining? Flea markets and vintage-clothing shops are brilliant sources for dress-up clothes. I have a collection of lovely festive dresses from the forties and fifties; some are only for fancier occasions, but many become constants in my wardrobe. My favorite fabrics are rayon, cotton, and silk taffeta, and I keep an eye open for dresses with pretty ruffles or pleats. Hats also can be fun; they don't need to be dramatic, especially if you keep them small.

Vintage tea dresses—cotton, rayon, and moiré. Fun for dress-up. Or everyday wear.

CHINA MATCHING & REPLACEMENT

One of the beauties of collecting and using old china is that it can be inexpensive, particularly if you use mismatched pieces, which can be aesthetically great. It is much cheaper to buy a dinner service that is incomplete. If you want to complete it, or if you find a piece that you love so much you want more of it, you can use a china matching and replacement service.

There are many such services, and it is not difficult to find one that specializes in the make and pattern that you are seeking; look in your Yellow Pages for a local service. The larger companies with 800 numbers often advertise in magazines, or can be found on the Internet.

Replacements, Ltd. in Greensboro, North Carolina, has the largest inventory of old and new china (as well as silver, crystal, and collectibles). Their inventory of six million pieces includes more than 120,000 patterns. They also offer:

- gift certificates
- lay-away plans
- a search service—they will look for a rare piece and call you when they find it
- collect calling

- showroom
- guided tours
- catalog
- Web site
- free pattern printouts with prices

Some of the smaller, more specialized companies also offer one or more of these services.

Above: I buy plates for what they look like, but I think the marks on the back, which tell when and where they were made, are beautiful too. I love the way the colors, lettering, and crests sometimes have blended and blurred into the glaze.

Opposite: A fun, festive rather gaudy gold cup.

The ornament of a house

is the friends who frequent it.

—Ralph Waldo Emerson

Flowers are one of the greatest and most satis-fying indulgences of life. I love those growing in my garden, and I love arranging cut flowers; I enjoy setting out my collection of vases and creating arrangements for every room in the house. I even enjoy it when I am so busy that I haven't time to arrange my flowers the day I get them, and so they sit in large, cool buckets for a day, or sometimes even two, luxurious and beautiful in their bunched profusion.

My garden is an explosion of texture and color, perfectly suited to the grounds: elegant morning glories and romantic roses, the tropical splendor of honey-suckle and the color explosion of wisteria, all amid lush foliage and the dappled sunlight admitted by the trees. And I cut nearly everything for indoors—from hydrangeas and camellias to the azalea blossoms that I sprinkle on my daughter's breakfast tray.

Opposite: A silver pitcher, found at a flea market, full of sweet peas. So fragile, so precious.

I have a large collection of vases, acquired over the years at flea markets and secondhand shops. Sometimes a treasure from my china cupboard—a chipped jug or a teapot that has lost its lid—will find a new life among my vases. I have one or two clear-glass vases whose shape is useful but whose appearance is a little dull; these I make more interesting by filling the bottom of the vases with colorful shells or stones.

I have flowers all over my house, in all the expected and unexpected places, all carefully placed, and never centered—I prefer them off to one side. Roses, peonies, hydrangeas, sweet peas, and tulips are among my favorites. I particularly like putting oversized flowers such as roses or peonies in small vases and clustering them in groups.

My children have grown up with lots of flowers in the house. Jake used to resist my attempts to include his room when placing my flower arrangements, but from time to time he'll accept a brown vase with white flowers, usually tulips or roses. Over the years he has learned the names of quite a few flowers—knowledge that may come in handy someday. When I take Lily her ritual tray of tea and cookies every night, I always put a flower on the tray; now that she is old enough, she brings me little treats on trays too, always with a flower.

Above right: English cream pottery. A small grouping is lovely.

Opposite: A boring glass vase. I fill the bottom with pretty stuff. In this vase I have put pink and white glass marbles and shells.

Above: Luscious flowers: hydrangeas and ranunculus. I took the hydrangea blooms from a really inexpensive plant; once cut, the flowers lasted about three weeks and I still have the original plant in my garden!

Opposite: Monochromatic: white flowers, white shells.

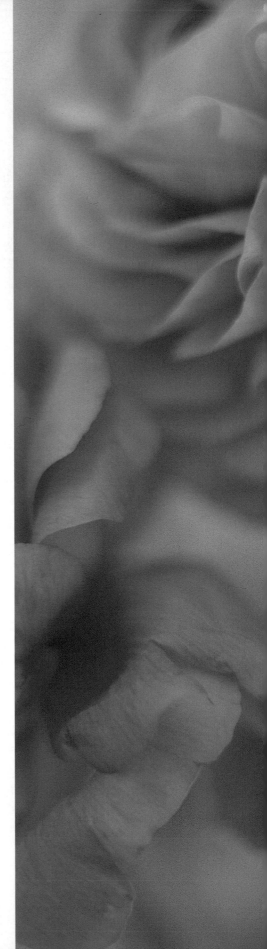

Having a house full of flowers is one of the great pleasures of life, and even if you don't grow your own, they don't have to be expensive. It is only necessary to shop carefully, and to look after your flowers once you've brought them home.

For me, a rose has the most varied life span, beautiful as a bud, in full bloom, and even when overblown as the petals start to drop. A bunch of roses is lovely, but so is a single bloom in a bud vase. My garden is planted with mature old-fashioned roses, and there is nothing more special than picking my own flowers. When I bought my house many of the roses were yellow, but my gardener Laura swapped them for colors that belong in my palette.

Above: A slightly imperfect gold-and-cream pitcher. The water bleeds through, marking the china, but the pitcher is still watertight for flowers.

Roses from La Loma farm, owned by my lovely neighbor Kristi Stevens.

A bearded iris.

Part of a Japanese streamer. I love the faded and irregular colors, the floppy folds.

Tiny flowers on a delicate plate echo the pale cloth underneath.

A wonderful paper bag full of
rich old velvet and silk flowers. Decorative, or I may find
them a specific use.

v i s i o n

Flowers are not only one of the great pleasures of my life, but their inspiration is a central part of Shabby Chic. Their influence can be seen in everything I design—there is very little in the fabrics, bedding, decoration, and colors I use that doesn't somehow come from flowers. The inspiration boards all over my house have flowers and floral references on them; my china, my dresses, my decorations are all floral. It is a rare moment that a flower, in some form, is not in my line of vision.

Top: I found this not very Shabby Chic throw pillow at a flea market. The design and dramatic size of the flower became the inspiration for a Shabby Chic fabric pattern called "pale bunch."

Opposite: My deck is a perfect place to review some artwork for a new Shabby Chic fabric—out-of-doors, close to the original inspiration!

GETTING FULL VALUE OUT OF FLOWERS

- It is not always necessary to buy flowers at a florist. If you are careful that they are fresh, good flowers can be bought at a corner market, or even a supermarket. You may be fortunate enough to have a farmers' market nearby, and these are good sources for seasonal flowers.

- A small quantity of flowers imaginatively used (in a cluster of bud vases?) can be as effective as a larger bunch.

- Choose cut flowers that have a long life. For example, a rose will last many more days than an iris. Hydrangeas and orchids are also flowers I love that can last a long time.

- To extend the life of cut flowers, trim the stem of each daily, either cutting under warm water or replacing the flower in the vase quickly. Snip off all leaves or thorns below water level. Slice the stems at an angle using a paring knife, not scissors, which can crush the stem.

- Use the sachet that comes with the flowers, or bleach, to keep bacteria out of the water.

- Change the water every day, and then wash the vase thoroughly after you throw out the flowers.

Opposite: The green frilly neck of this vase is, to my eye, beautiful. A collar of green for my silk roses.

accents

Top: A beaded butterfly and an Indian bracelet.

Bottom: Velvet fruit, ceramic flowers, fabric butterflies.

Opposite: Another of my inspiration boards.

Paper butterflies.

helping hands

Ted, Syl, Kevin, and Chris—I couldn't
have done it without them.

There is nothing like a dream to create the future.

—Victor Hugo

Resource Guide

SHABBY CHIC CORPORATE OFFICES
6330 Arizona Circle
Los Angeles, CA 90045
*For information on other stores
carrying Shabby Chic products,
please call (310) 258–0660.*

SHABBY CHIC
BY RACHEL ASHWELL STORES
1013 Montana Avenue
Santa Monica, CA 90403
(310) 394–1974

46 East Superior Avenue
Chicago, IL 60611
(312) 649–0080

SHABBY CHIC STORES
93 Greene Street
New York, NY 10012
(212) 274–9842

3075 Sacramento Street
San Francisco, CA 94115
(415) 771–3881

LA LOMA ROSES
Kristi Stevens
(805) 386–8002
*Wholesale only
(all roses in book)*

TILE EMPORIUM
(310) 393–0499
Tiles in bathroom and swimming pool

RESTORATION HARDWARE
(310) 458–7992
Reproduction hardware

LIZ'S ANTIQUE HARDWARE
(323) 939–4403
Authentic hardware

KEVIN BABINEAU CONSTRUCTION
(310) 456–6342
House contractor

AMERICAN QUALITY PLUMBING
Ted Beason
(310) 456–7220
*Plumbing contractor specializing
in authentic plumbing*

GARDEN VISION
Laura Knauss
(310) 457–4944
Landscape designer

*Kovel's New Dictionary of
Marks: Pottery and Porcelain,
1850 to the Present*
Ralph and Terry Kovel
(New York: Crown, 1986)
China marking reference book

REPLACEMENTS, LTD.
1089 Knox Road
P.O. Box 26029
Greensboro, NC 27420
(800) REPLACE
*China, crystal,
silver replacement*

CHINA REPLACEMENTS
2263 Williams Creek Drive
High Ridge, MO 63049
(800) 562–2650

BYEGONE CHINA MATCH
1225 West 34th Street North
Witchita, KS 67204
(316) 838–6010

The
GOLDEN TOMORROW

Today is the golden Tomorrow
that you dreamed of Yesterday —
and so it will be until the end
of Time. This day, then, is your
Day of Opportunity !

NOTES

NOTES

NOTES